TWAYNE'S WORLD AUTHORS SERIES

A Survey of the World's Literature

Sylvia E. Bowman, Indiana University

GENERAL EDITOR '

ARGENTINA

John P. Dyson, Indiana University

EDITOR

Eduardo Mallea

TWAS 433

Eduardo Mallea

EDUARDO MALLEA

By H. ERNEST LEWALD

University of Tennessee

TWAYNE PUBLISHERS
A DIVISION OF G. K. HALL & CO., BOSTON

Library of Congress Cataloging in Publication Data

Lewald, Herald Ernest.
  Eduardo Mallea.

  (Twayne's world authors series; TWAS 433: Argentina)
  Bibliography: p. 113–15.
  Includes index.
  1. Mallea, Eduardo, 1903–   2. Authors,
Argentine—20th century—Biography.
PQ7797.M225Z73   863 [B]   76-44804
ISBN 0-8057-6273-6

MANUFACTURED IN THE UNITED STATES OF AMERICA

To Ann, with all my love

Contents

About the Author

H. Ernest Lewald has lived and studied in Germany, Uruguay and Argentina. He received his Ph.D. in Spanish at the University of Minnesota and has taught at Georgia Tech., Carleton College, Purdue and the California State College at Fullerton. He is presently Professor of Romance Languages and Comparative Literature as well as Chairman of Latin American Studies at the University of Tennessee in Knoxville. His main publications include *Buenos Aires: retrato de una sociedad a través de su literatura* (Houghton Mifflin, 1968); *Argentina, análisis y autoanálisis* (Sudamericana, 1969); *The Cry of Home: Cultural Nationalism and the Modern Writer* (Univ. of Tennessee Press, 1972); and *Latinoamérica: sus culturas y sociedades* (McGraw-Hill, 1973). He has also published many articles on River Plate literature and culture.

Preface

While there exist several book-length studies on the work of Eduardo Mallea, such as John H. R. Polt's published dissertation, *The Writings of Eduardo Mallea* (1959), Carmen Rivelli's *Eduardo Mallea* (1969), Myron Lichtblau's *El arte estilístico de Eduardo Mallea*, a fine thematic study by Herbert Gillessen called *Themes, Images, and Motifs in the Work of Eduardo Mallea* (*Themen, Bilder und Motive im Werk Eduardo Malleas*. 1966), and a biography by Oscar Villordo published by EUDEBA in Buenos Aires, a systematic study of the man and his work was indeed in order.

The advantage of a thorough study of a writer like Mallea is obvious. It becomes possible to trace the origin and development of themes, characterization, and style, evaluate influences, contrast the writer's position vis-à-vis national and international trends, and estimate his standing as an author. Due to the large number of volumes produced by Mallea, this study of the trajectorylike character of his work has been determined by a chronological progression.

Eduardo Mallea entered the Argentine literary scene in 1926 with a book of stories called *Stories for a Desperate Englishwoman* (*Cuentos para una inglesa desesperada*) that produced a strong impact locally. A prolific writer, he has since published over thirty novels and books of essays besides short pieces between 1926 and 1971. In his role as fiction writer and essayist, he has dominated the Argentine world of letters in the 1930s and 1940s. In an era still affected by social realism, Mallea began to forge a very personal expression that in its highest form carries the seeds of an ontological awareness that was later cultivated by French existentialists and their followers. At the same time he was able to combine themes explored in his fiction with those prevalent in his essays. What stands out here is the search for the vital forces that in his eyes had laid the basis for the genuine Argentine culture and that had become altered by the appearance of millions of European immigrants and covered by layers of urban congestion and a false way of life.

Reserved, refined, and solitary, Mallea has evolved a *Weltanschauung* that has incorporated values belonging to his father and his era, an influence that has made itself felt often in style and subject matter. Mallea's predilect characters reflect their creator. Cerebral, hermetic, and anguished, they yearn to transcend their sterile condition in order to communicate and commune. In the final instance, Mallea's search for the authentic Argentina is intertwined with his search to discover his true self, often in the guise of his protagonists. Thus his symbols, themes, and types recur and become redrawn and redefined as his work progresses.

As editor of the "Literary Supplement" of *La Nación,* Argentina's finest newspaper, and as a member in good standing of the Sur-Sudamericana-Florida group made up of such writers as Jorge Luis Borges and Manuel Mujica Laínez, Mallea formed part of the literary establishment and exercised a considerable influence on the Argentine scene until his departure in 1955, when, in the post-*peronista* era, he accepted the position to represent his country at the UNESCO headquarters in Paris for two years. Although the literary panorama has naturally changed in the last fifteen years, now partly dominated by cultivators of the "new novel" such as Julio Cortázar, Ernest Sábato, and perhaps Manuel Puig, Mallea remains a force within the context of the Argentine novel and essay, and his best works enjoy an unprecedented success in his homeland as well as abroad.

Acknowledgments

I would like to acknowledge here above all Mallea's efforts to give me a personal orientation with regard to a number of his works. Only too often do critics venture to invent reasons and motivations that serve as false explanations for the creation of a given piece of fiction. Mallea's preparation of a sixteen-page, single-spaced manuscript, simply called "Notas para Lewald," has helped me immeasurably with my biographical and textual interpretations. Similarly, my interviews with him have aided in my comprehension of some of his work. Finally, I wish to acknowledge the good services of María Elena Gaviola, widow of the well-known Argentine novelist Manuel Gálvez, and H. A. Murena, a great man of letters and a friend, for their encouragement and helpful suggestions concerning the Argentine world of letters. The translations of excerpts from Mallea's works as well as of those belonging to criticism written in Spanish and German are my own.

H. ERNEST LEWALD

University of Tennessee

Chronology

1903   Eduardo Mallea born on August 14, in Bahía Blanca, a seaport on the Atlantic in Argentina.
1907   First trip to Europe with parents and older brother.
1910   Enters British prep school in Bahía Blanca; exposed to many children of Northern European descent and culture.
1916   The father gives up his medical practice and moves family to Buenos Aires.
1920   Enters law school at the University of Buenos Aires where he makes friends interested in literature.
1921–   Neglects law studies and becomes involved with literary
1923   magazines. Publishes *Revista de América* with Luis Saslawsky.
1926   Publishes *Stories for a Desperate Englishwoman (Cuentos para una inglesa desesperada)* containing short pieces, some of which had been printed earlier.
1927   Abandons law career and takes a job as a correspondent for *La Nación*, Argentina's foremost newspaper.
1928   Travels to Europe to represent *La Nación* at the Olympic Games in Amsterdam. Back in Buenos Aires he translates some of Joyce's work with Jorge Luis Borges.
1931   Becomes editor of the "Literary Supplement" of *La Nación*, a key position in the world of Argentine letters.
1934   Travels to Europe and gives lectures in Rome and Milan; also
1935   Publishes the novel *European Nocturn (Nocturno europeo)* and the long essay *Knowledge and Expression of Argentina. Conscimiento y expressión de la Argentina).*
1936   Publishes a collection of short stories under the title *The City on the Motionless River (La ciudad junto al río inmóvil).*
1937   Publishes his most famous collection of essays, *History of an Argentine Passion (Historia de una pasión argentina).*
1938   Publishes *Fiesta in November (Fiesta en noviembre).*
1940   Elected president of the Sociedad Argentina de Escritores, the writers' guild to which almost all major authors belonged. Publishes *The Bay of Silence (La bahía de silencio).*

1941   Death of his father, who was a major influence on Eduardo. Publishes *All Green Shall Perish (Todo verdor perecerá).*

1944   Marries Helena Muñóz Larreta, member of one of Argentina's oldest and most prestigious families.

1945   Awarded the Primer Premio Nacional de Letras.

1946   Awarded the Gran Premio de Honor of the Sociedad Argentina de Escritores.

1950   Publishes *The Enemies of the Soul (Los enemigos del alma).*

1953   Publishes *Chaves* and *The Waiting Room (La sala de espera).*

1955   After the fall of the Perón regime, represents Argentina at UNESCO in Paris. Gives up the editorship of the "Literary Supplement" in *La Nación. The Waiting Room (La sala de espera)* awarded the Premio Casavalle.

1956   Attends UNESCO conference in New Delhi, India.

1957   Publishes the novel *Sindbad (Simbad).* Returns to Argentina.

1958   Publishes *Possession (Posesión).*

1961–   Publishes *Crossings (Las Travesías).*
1962

1966   Publishes a volume of three short novels under the title *Resentment (El resentimiento).*

1967   Publishes *The Ice Ship (La barca de hielo),* a collection of nine stories narrated by one protagonist.

1968   Awarded the Forti Glori prize. Publishes *The Net (La red),* a collection of fiction and essays.

1969   Publishes the novel *The Penultimate Door (La penúltima puerta).*

1970   Awarded the Gran Premio Nacional de las Artes, previously given only twice in the literary category.

1971   Publishes *Gabriel Andaral* and *Sad Skin of the Universe (Triste piel del universo),* a novel that takes place in India and closes a trilogy.

CHAPTER 1

The Formative Period

I *The Early Years*

WHILE biographical references to a writer's formative period happen to constitute an almost obligatory element, in the case of Eduardo Mallea such references carry a special weight. Certain family relationships and cultural influences turn into constants that become keys in the evaluation of some of his major and recurring themes that persist throughout a literary career that by now extends through five decades.

He was born in Bahía Blanca, Argentina on August 14, 1903, into the family of Narciso S. Mallea as the second of three boys. The Malleas belong to one of Argentina's old colonial families that traces its ancestry to a Spanish nobleman, one Juan Eugenio de Mallea, who founded the town of San Juan along the western frontier close to Chile, today a very important city and capital of a province by the same name. The Malleas achieved prominence in San Juan and were repeatedly mentioned in the provincial chronicles of a distant relative, Domingo Faustino Sarmiento, one of the nation's greatest political and literary figures. Narciso S. Mallea, a contemporary of President Sarmiento, reversed the migratory trend and went eastward to study medicine in Buenos Aires while hundreds of thousands of European immigrants moved westward to find a place under the sun on the open prairies. After practicing medicine under the most primitive conditions and even teaching in rural areas of the huge Buenos Aires province, he married a student of his, one Manuela Aztiria, daughter of a Basque landowner. The doctor then decided to settle down in Bahía Blanca, a seaport in the extreme south of the province, a halfway point between the River Plate and lifeless, cold Patagonia, a town strongly influenced by English and German elements. Here he practiced surgery, took on the duties of directing a hospital, and received out-patients in his spacious home.

But the good doctor proved to be more than just a practicing physician. In the latter part of the nineteenth century the intellectual and social orientation of Argentine upper-class families, especially in the closed circuits of provincial towns, was still deeply rooted in classical traditions and mannerisms. This orientation had mainly originated in the eighteenth-century salon life and its rational outlook that displaced the Spanish intellectual heritage in Latin America during the Age of Independence, from Hidalgo in Mexico to Bolivar in Great Colombia and Moreno in the River Plate. The intellectual life in towns like San Juan or Bahía Blanca at the turn of the century was usually centered around informal meetings held by teachers, medical doctors, practicing lawyers, or high public officials at a café, a gentlemen's club, or someone's salon. The participants would consciously feel part of an elite whose roots reached as far back as the Renaissance concept of the ideal courtier: the *complete* man who knows how to combine the spheres of science, belles-lettres, and politics.

Dr. Mallea proved to be an accomplished exponent of this genteel tradition. His library held a remarkable collection of European authors, and he spent several hours daily there reading and writing. Early in the mornings he liked to practice with his fencing master, and afternoons he spent some time with his French instructor. His knowledge of Dante, Machiavelli, and Molière was almost proverbial. Whenever free from his medical duties he loved to discuss literature, history, and art in a circle of friends that resembled a mixture of the French salon and that time-honored institution known as the Spanish *tertulia*. An active politician, he joined the emergent populist party, then called Unión Cívica Radical, and expressed his accumulated enlightenment in a variety of articles on the need for social reform that appeared in newspapers at that time and were considered radical by the conservative element. In fact, the vehemence of his attacks on the existing socioeconomic conditions, then mainly manipulated by an entrenched oligarchy made up of landed gentry, brought him a chance to try out his fencing skill on the "field of honor" with members of the Partido Conservador, and he was wounded on one of those occasions.

Many of Dr. Mallea's avocations and exploits were later to be blended into a glowing texture that represented memories of this past in the mind of his son Eduardo. His mother hardly shares Dr. Mallea's limelight when it comes to reminiscences or the evocation of early childhood. Next to the portrayal of his father as the almost romantic figure of rural medicine and later the brilliant and inspiring mentor, the mother is drawn in a rather pale fashion. Thus Eduardo Mallea tells Victoria Ocampo in their dialogue: ". . . the opposite of my father, she possessed a weak and vulnerable character. She overlooked our wrongdoings and lamented the harsh paternal discipline."[1]

When Eduardo was four years old his father took the family to Europe and they visited Paris, the obligatory mecca of educated Latin Americans. Although Eduardo's memories of the family visits to the forest near Fontainebleau and the crooked, narrow streets running through Montmartre faded away before they could leave a lasting impression,[2] his first European experience amounted to a sort of preamble that set the direction for a framework in which the writer would be operating for the duration of his literary career. This preamble was to be reinforced when, upon returning to Bahía Blanca, Eduardo was placed in a local English grammar school, run by a formidable Australian, one Mrs. Hilton, who tried her hand at having the students equate discipline with Anglo-Saxon civic virtue.

As Eduardo's childhood progressed he began to participate more fully in the routine of family life. At the center stood, overwhelmingly, the figure of Dr. Narciso S. Mallea, which was to be so vividly accounted for in the autobiographical chapter of *History of an Argentine Passion (Historia de una pasión argentina)*, possibly his single most important piece of writing. The son records: "My father belonged to a breed of men that possessed an iron morality and who usually make their appearance at a time when a new nation is in the making. . . . [Thus] since my earliest childhood I became used to admiring his mental vigor, his total honesty, his generosity, education, and extraordinary courage of standing by his convictions, all implemented with great physical courage."[3]

Not too surprisingly, Eduardo reflects that "our lives—my mother, my older brother, and I—were centered, almost silently, around my Father";[4] and certain repeated descriptions employed by the writer create a meaningful composite profile that was to be inherited by the son. Some of the salient personal traits are to be " . . . refined, elegant [in one's] expression, genteel, generous, vehement, enveloped by an air of dignity, precise in his usage of words and syntax. . . ."[5]

Of course, there were outside influences on young Eduardo, but they carried a sedate and negative quality and stemmed largely from whatever ambiance Bahía Blanca had to offer. There were the quiet, blond boys and auburn-haired girls of the English colony, the windswept bay where freighters stopped on their way up and down the coast, and the view of the solitary pampas during those grey winter days, all combining to create monotonous and lonely surroundings for a rather timid and introspective child. Eduardo actually found the other children's games trite and their mentality pretty savage; and he much preferred spending his free time listening to his father's coachman conjuring up stories from an already remote frontier life.[6] Thus the boy fell back on his family circle, avidly absorbing a past filled with tales about the father's meeting with President Sarmiento or other great figures out of Argentina's history or reliving episodes from the father's youth until they all became an inner reality.

How much Dr. Mallea was responsible for the shaping of his son's *Weltanschauung* can be derived from the fact that in 1916 he decided to abandon his medical career and hospital position in Bahía Blanca in order to supervise the children's education in Buenos Aires where the oldest son had already begun his studies at the university. There in a spacious apartment at 912 Esmeralda Street in the heart of downtown, the good doctor held weekly literary meetings attended by his son's friends and classmates.

As young Eduardo went through the upper grades of the Colegio Nacional, an elite high school structured along the lines of the classical French *lycée*, his interest in studying actually decreased, but he continued to receive parental guidelines for his intellectual and artistic orientation. Many years later Eduardo Mallea confided to Victoria Ocampo that he never ceased to admire his father's personal philosophy of life and energy—the latter defined as the will to act virtuously—fully realizing that his filial imitation would always fall short of perfection.[7] He continued his secondary education but found that the Argentine teachers hardly measured up to the standards and competence exhibited by those at the British school in Bahía Blanca. To him they were indolent physicians or lawyers who came to teach their class in mathematics or grammar and quickly left again. The only two teachers who made a lasting impression on him were Mr. François in French and Mr. Wilkins in physics, hardly two *criollo* names. Looking back at his highschool years Mallea sees

himself in a light that, on the one hand, made him out to be a
continuation of his father's personality and, on the other, showed
him to possess qualities present in most outstanding writers: sensitivity, compassion, and imagination. In his "Notas" he states:

I showed what you might call my "literary nature" at an early age. I read a
lot of Dickens, Chateaubriand, Hugo, and Turgenev . . . and when I did
not lose myself in the world of fiction I felt the strange sensation of suffering
for almost anything that happened. Being overly sensitive and compassion-
ate, I was moved to tears by any misfortune that I witnessed or was told
about. But this propensity also had the effect of making me overreact to any
situation seemingly involving a lack of respect or consideration as far as
myself was concerned; and I began to feel victimized.[8]

This sensitivity and self-centered stance precede his mood of anguish and even melancholia that become so apparent in his later
fiction. In retrospect he was to see himself as a creature molded by
this anguish, and he hoped to develop a more resilient disposition to
shrug off his pangs of adversity and attacks of self-pity.[9] But quite
obviously Mallea would never be able to solve the ontological problem of rejecting the projection of his idealized self. Yet, he did
speculate on the advantages of being a very different type of personality, one endowed with much less self-pity or autoanalysis and with
more force of action, inner decisiveness, and a more physically
oriented frame of mind.[10] With the passage of time, of course, came
the realization that "one is simply what one is and not what one
wants to be," with the addendum that "under the best of circumstances one may even measure up to one's possibilities,
whether one likes them or not."[11]
    As his teenage period progressed, his literary interests expanded
while, at the same time, the urge to do creative writing made itself
felt. The matter of literary influences becomes an obligatory topic;
but, while in a number of instances critics have successfully discovered and explored specific influences on writers, in Mallea's case
such a task would look fairly hopeless. Several accounts of his favorite readings are in print, but such lists remain far from conclusive as
to specific impacts or trends. For instance, Juan Manuel Topete and
Carmen Rivelli both mention a number of philosophers, novelists,
and poets by simply referring to Mallea's allusion to these men in
the final pages of his *History of an Argentine Passion*, although

Mallea never stated explicitly that he read or assimilated their basic thoughts or accepted their positions. At any rate, we find what can be considered an annotated bibliography: "William Blake and his prophetic spirit; Rimbaud, wandering around the streets of Charleroi to escape the moral fraud of his society: Kierkegaard and his anguish; Nietzsche the aphorist and eternal sufferer; Novalis, the composer of *Thoughts to the Night* whose love and death find a common poetic ground; and later St. Augustine with his *Confessions* followed by the mystic exponents of the precursors: Santa Teresa and San Juan de la Cruz."[12]

When Topete adds a list of preferred authors that include such widely divergent figures as Marcel Proust, James Joyce, Miguel de Unamuno, Mariano José de Larra, Franz Kafka, and Liam O'Flaherty,[13] it becomes difficult to establish direct contacts between Mallea and these writers. However, Topete ventures to trace definite influences when pointing out that Mallea owes Proust his detailed descriptions and that Angel Ganivet helped him to use the concept of a spiritual geography in his search for the true Argentina.[14] No doubt, the passage of time changes perspectives and even alters former certainties. In his dialogue with Victoria Ocampo, Mallea remembers that his favorite authors and works in his formative period were "Conan Doyle, *David Copperfield*, *Vanity Fair*, *Wuthering Heights*, de Maupassant, Bret Harte, all of Tolstoi, Balzac, Flaubert, the early H. G. Wells, *Robinson Crusoe*, *Don Quijote*, and all the prose and poetry of Edgar Allan Poe."[15] This *revised* list of 1969 bears truly no resemblance to the one included in his *History of an Argentine Passion*.

To assess the true impact of authors and works on a future writer in his formative years is at best a risky business, since it involves not only an extremely difficult biographical accuracy but also involves a deep knowledge of his intellectual and emotive assimilation, a process usually not even noticed by the writer himself. It actually profits little to look for genuine literary influences when examining his first serious effort, the stories and vignettes that make up the volume entitled *Stories for a Desperate Englishwoman (Cuentos para una inglesa desesperada)*. While the influence of *modernismo* on this work has been pointed out, one looks, however, in vain for an acknowledged debt to Darío and company on any of the established lists of influences. Perhaps one should make a point of observation concerning a negative element in his literary formation, namely, the almost total absence of Argentine or even Latin American prose writers and poets.

Upon reaching full adolescence Mallea discovered the world of the female; but here too his introspection and hermetic nature allowed for a more cerebral than social or physical interaction. Perhaps the cultural milieu of Argentine urban society about 1920 influenced his apparently infrequent involvement with the opposite sex. Buenos Aires at that point in history combined the physical structure of Paris with a social climate of a frontier boom town where men, immigrants from all corners of Europe as well as rural workers from the Argentine provinces, came to look for work and outnumbered women by a drastic percentage. It was the era of the red-light district, the "French" parlor, and the waterfront bars that gave Buenos Aires a worldwide notoriety reflected in such works as *Road to Buenos Aires* (*Le chemin de Buenos Aires*, 1972) by the French writer Albert Londres. In Argentina the bestseller by Manuel Gálvez, *Nacha Regules* (1919) and a little later the volume of essays by Raúl Scalabrini Ortiz, *The Man who Stands Alone and Waits* (*El hombre que está solo y espera*, 1931) both point to the sexual rapaciousness of the male as well as to the hermetic mood of this male-dominated city. Inextricably coupled to this unbalanced pattern of human relations we find the extensive practice of a laissez-faire capitalism with its sweatshop techniques and labor exploitation that included economic pressure or material temptations for lower-class girls to trade sex for comfort, a theme so abundantly dramatized in *Nacha Regules*.

For the young Mallea the salient social issues and class confrontations fictionalized by a number of Argentine prose writers from Manuel Gálvez to David Viñas, both of whom, for instance, focused on the "Tragic Week" in 1919 when dozens of workers died by police bullets, went largely unnoticed. His private world was apparently not touched by the immediacy of the political or social issues involving the existing and numerous proletariat in the semi-industrialized Argentine capital and the efforts to secure better living conditions.

His social relations were based on a pattern established by a very traditional and genteel form of family life and the introvert habits of a young man who has learned a wealth of details about life and has consequently formed an approach to life based upon this book knowledge. Thus his first adventurous steps toward the eternal female are couched in somewhat vicarious terms. He writes: "As a good novelistic hero I dreamed of being the idol of all these little shopgirls whom I saw or at times followed on the streets of Buenos Aires and now saw myself as a sentimental seducer of young ladies instead of the scourge of evildoers. I reveled in the thought of being selected by one of these girls with the anticipation of playing the eternally faithful hero."[16]

In real life, however, he knew himself to be timid and less than convincing in the role of the ardent lover, propensities that play a decisive role in the fashioning of his first literary efforts that are collected in *Stories for a Desperate Englishwoman* that appeared in 1926 when Mallea was already twenty-three years old.

Luckily for our young sentimentalist, his personal obligations were deeply anchored in the social circle so carefully laid out by his father, and thus he was able to relegate his amorous intentions to the level of occasional adventures that seemed insignificant enough as not to be mentioned in his self-appraisals that fill a goodly number of pages in such works as *History of an Argentine Passion, The Inner War (La guerra interior)*, or his dialogue with Victoria Ocampo. Later he was to view these formative years in Buenos Aires as rather tranquil ones in which he experienced a healthy share of happiness based on the fact that his early world comprised a good home, interesting guests, an undemanding highschool curriculum, and a few personal friends. If he felt insufficient it was due to an unfulfilled need to prove himself to be worthy of the love and affection of those who lived in this inner circle. Probably he experienced a very strong urge to perceive and behave aesthetically, that is, to evolve a life-style in which such characteristics as generosity, bonhomie, and disinterest would set the dominant tone, allowing him to personify a desired image for the benefit of his friends and relatives. He craved recognition but always within a carefully constructed social context; and, like most, he also felt the disappointment of not measuring up to his own projected expectations as far as talent and craft are concerned. Perhaps the single most significant conclusion to be drawn from this period is that Mallea had little use for possessions or ideas unless they could be transposed to a level of human need; but, at the same time, his interpretation of human need was severely conditioned by models that reached out from the past. He dreamed for years about owning Charles Dickens' Gadshil Place, a dream which materialized years later.

II *The Literary Scene*

After graduating from the Colegio Nacional Mallea entered the University of Buenos Aires to study law, as his older brother had done. He was enrolled for about three years, but his scant interest in this field, so popular with many Latin American students up to this day, prompted him to drop out as he felt more and more attracted to the world of belles-lettres and its varied possibilities. In 1921 he had come into contact with a group of liberal-arts students and young literati who felt that the time was ripe for exploring new literary horizons and for pooling their efforts in the publication of a magazine. Being eighteen at the time, the excitement of collaborating in a magazine that could be considered avant-guard and elitist at the same time fitted Mallea's orientation. Actually, Mallea contributed only a modest amount of writing or editing, but the constant meetings with this group, held informally and with great enthusiasm and at times accompanied by readings or recitations, contained all the elements of the traditional literary *tertulia,* so widely and effectively used by the *modernistas* a generation earlier.

Among the participants of the magazine, entitled simply *Revista de América,* were Juan Carlos Erro, Luis Saslavsky, and Leonardo and Enrique de Vedia, the latter acting as managing editor. While the personal and literary temperament of the collaborators showed individual differences, the common denominator was furnished by a kind of *arielista Weltanschauung* that placed aesthetic and ontological considerations above a social or political awareness. Erro, for instance, advocated the aristocracy of mind and the triumph of spiritual over materialistic life, championed by the Uruguayan José Enrique Rodó, creator of *Ariel* in 1900. All in all, the group represented a continuation of different European and Latin American currents whose essence contained a preoccupation with art for art's sake and that influenced the two most important literary publications of the 1920s in Argentina, *Martín Fierro* and *Proa.* Understandably, this participation gave Mallea enough of a taste to decide against a legal career in spite of his father's serious objections; and he made up his mind to confide in the muses. In his second and possibly most significant novel, *The Bay of Silence (La bahía de silencio),* the *Revista de América* is called *Enough (Basta),* and the group of young literati reappears under different names, in order to renovate, among other things, literature—once again.

But Mallea's earliest literary activities were not confined to the magazine alone. His very first short story, "The Amazon" ("La Amazona"), had been accepted in *Caras y Caretas*, a well-known weekly to which the most prestigious national figures contributed. His story "Cynthia" was first published in *Revista de América;* and the next two, "Sonata of Solitude" ("Sonata de Soledad") and "Neel," were included in the "Sunday Supplement" of Argentina's most outstanding daily newspaper, *La Nación*. Here, then, began a lifelong association with *La Nación* and the Mitres, another patrician Argentine family who still own the paper; and Mallea was later to take over the editorship of the important "Literary Supplement" of *La Nación* for more than two decades, a position that gave him the power and prestige to be a decisive influence on the Argentine literary scene.

In the meantime Mallea began to amplify his literary contacts and by 1926 had established his basic roots in the complex and elusive milieu of Buenos Aires, the sole major *focus* of cultural, literary and publishing activities for the River Plate nations. This milieu had a cosmopolitan flavor of its own. In the 1920s Buenos Aires was a city of two million people and constituted the most European enclave in a continent still filled with unconquered jungles, mountains, and deserts, Indian communities in the sierras, and descendants of African slaves along the tropical coastal strips. At least one out of every two people walking on the streets of the Argentine capital was foreign born, and the general public followed religiously any political development occurring in the Old World, from the collapse of Imperial Germany and Austria to the rise of communism in Russia and the beginnings of fascism in Italy.

In the intellectual and artistic circles the orientation toward the other side of the Atlantic proved equally powerful and pervasive. Ernest Ansermet arrived to direct the philharmonic orchestra and perform Stravinsky, Schönberg, and Hindemith; Anna Pavlova and her *corps de ballet* came to the Colón Opera House, which was built on a most lavish scale; Pirandello's *Six Characters in Search of an Author* became a huge success; a Van Gogh and Cézanne exposition drew large crowds; the Prince of Wales visited the pampas and fell off his polo pony, and a twentyish Jorge Luis Borges returned from Europe with a poetic manifesto in his valise.

This last event contributed greatly to the establishment of a "new sensitivity" *(la nueva sensibilidad)* which consisted mainly of importing the latest avant-gardism from Paris or Madrid. Borges' *ultraismo*, as other *isms* of the years following World War I, represented a renewed attempt to make a case for the artist and poet as a supremely free and original interpreter of the universe and its multiple manifestations. *Ultraismo*, then, placed due emphasis on aesthetic expression at the expense of the sociopolitical realities of the emergent Argentine nation and its incipient mass culture. Although *ultraismo* failed to take roots in Argentine soil, such writers as Jorge Luis Borges, Oliverio Girondo, and Enrique González Lanuza became very active in the important Martín Fierrista group and inspired its direction. This group, usually considered as the dominant influence on the Argentine literary milieu in the 1920s, produced a manifesto of its own, published in 1924, in which it defended cosmopolitanism and rejected nationalism in literature, especially the strictly regionalistic treatment that was prevalent in Latin American prose of the period. As González Lanuza was to write many years later, the short-lived Martín Fierro group "fluctuated between a romantic search for novelty and an obvious debt to the powerful emanation of Darío's *modernismo* and Leopoldo Lugones' *postmodernismo*."[17] The apex of the Martín Fierrista activities came when a quite large group got together for the dual purpose of paying tribute to Ricardo Güiraldes in 1926 and celebrating the success of his gaucho novel *Don Segundo Sombra*. While on the surface this masterpiece fits into the general category of what critics call "the novel of the land," Güiraldes' genius was able to use the traditional folkways and the cliché-ridden country language in a poetic way, injecting freshness and originality without, however, disturbing the local spirit or the country psychology of the characters. Young Mallea was among those attending the homage.

Although *Martín Fierro* ceased publication in 1927, its collaborators and sympathizers continued engaging in an amorphous interaction that later was given the name of the "Florida" group. The name was derived from the elegant shopping street in the heart of downtown Buenos Aires, and symbolized a basic continuity of the art-for-art's-sake orientation. At the same time, a countergroup developed that went under the name of "Boedo," a workers' district in another part of town. Its adherents, generally lesser known than their aesthete counterparts, found inspiration in a proletarian consciousness and the literary models of Emile Zola, Maxim Gorki, and the old master Dostoevski. By and large the "Boedo" prose reflected a *literatura de combate* carried out with a measure of didacticism, so often a by-product of socially inspired writing. Not surprisingly, the "Boedo" group found it necessary to take pot shots at "Florida" while the "enemy" frequently seemed much more nonchalant about the coexistence of both groups. Endowed with an acute critical sense, González Lanuza observed that the leftist press as well as the socially minded intellectuals did not need to condemn the "Martin Fierro" or "Florida" writers for trying to cultivate their own realities. Although the "Boedo" group was heterogeneous enough to count with a preexistentialist like Roberto Arlt whose stock has sharply risen over the years, one can easily find a good amount of ideological naiveté and defective writing among the rest.

The existence of both groups polarized to a large extent the ambitions and loyalties of the younger writer in the 1920s and 1930s. Although some of the original members of "Florida" and "Boedo" as well as some modern critics see this polarization as an overemphasized hiatus, the mainstream of Argentine literature has been traveling in either one of these two channels since the original division took place. "Florida," better endowed as to talent and resources, solidified into what became the establishment whose three vertexes were *La Nación*, the magazine *Sur*, founded by Victoria Ocampo in 1931, and the publishing house Sudamericana. "Boedo," on the other hand, could only master minor and short-lived magazines or poorly funded publishing firms such as Claridad. On the "Florida" side, the list of prominent writers extends from Borges to Cortázar, spanning almost half a century by now. The "Boedo" column records lesser names, from Arturo Cancela to David Viñas, and a history which is similar and equally meaningful.

III   Stories for a Desperate Englishwoman

From the beginnings of his career Mallea tossed his literary hat in with the Martín Fierro and the "Florida" faction, and later was to rise to one of the most prominent positions within the establishment. In 1926, then, appeared his first volume entitled *Stories for a Desperate Englishwoman*, a title that showed Mallea's predilection and inventiveness in naming his books and which was confirmed with each additional title. The first book presents a collection of stories and vignettes written and in some cases published between 1923 and 1926 when the author was in his early twenties. Today the evaluation of this fairly slender volume tends to regard it as an

Ausklang of the *modernista* period that in Argentina lingered on in figures like the poet Lugones who had helped Mallea place several of these short pieces with local magazines. The well-known Venezuelan writer Mariano Picón Salas certainly did not mind calling it a juvenile adventure of *modernista* inspiration.[18] José María Topete sees the stories of this volume as stylistic pirouettes that remind one of Darío's *Azul* but also constitute the promising beginning of a search for personal expression.[19]

In essence, the different characters that move through the pages of these stories are as cerebral as Darío's bourgeois king or Queen Mab; but this was to be expected. The world of young Eduardo was populated much more with fictional beings than real ones, and even the real ones were infused with a *Zeitgeist sui generis* fostered by Mallea's father, to whom the book is dedicated. In his first literary sally the young prose writer fashioned a world known to him largely from vicarious experiences. But to say that he achieved only a preamble to his more serious writing is to ignore certain constants that accompany Mallea in the form of inseparable archetypal models throughout his entire literary career. Thus *Stories for a Desperate Englishwoman* already throws a sharp focus on the elusive and eternal female, the autoanalytic and introverted male protagonist, the all-pervasive feeling of solitude and anguish on the part of the narrator, and a cosmopolitan, overly correct ambiance that seems to combine the worst features of upper-bourgeois life on both sides of the Atlantic.

Looking briefly at the various components of this volume, we find what Professor John Polt describes as "ample evidence of cosmopolitanism in style and mood [and] . . . the continual mention of foreign names and places."[20] We also find a forcible attempt to belabor a metaphysical dimension and see a great sensitivity toward style as a vehicle to convey the writer's mood and creative spirit, all of which places Mallea within the mainstream of the Martín Fierro and "Florida" *Dichterkreis*.

In "Arabella and I" ("Arabella y Yo") Mallea created a pastoral *tableau* in which the three protagonists constitute a variation of the traditional triangle as Arabella leaves her lover Axel for Virgilio, who sways her senses because of his naive and artless ways. There are many references to literary figures, the elegant and ceremonious milieu of the well situated, and English terms and locales. This background is blended with Arabella: blonde, haughty, snobbish, and insufferable,[21] to create an abstract world that, nevertheless, had a genuine meaning for Mallea himself.

"Sonata of Solitude" ("Sonata de soledad") shows the structure of a monologue in which a nameless Hamlet addresses his Ophelia. The setting seems vaguely European; a goodly number of learned references appear ranging from Cézanne to *Maria Chapdelaine*. The mood is meditative and the narration expository, although a few interspersed aphorisms such as "pity in women proves to be the dreariest of concessions" inject a satirical tone that could well be taken from the drawing room conversation of an Oscar Wilde play. The story proves to be largely cerebral, static, and lifeless.

"Neel" represents a vignette that is set in a Scandinavian fishing village. The triangle here is made up of Neel, the young fisherman Rabel, and the pastor Olmer. Responding strongly to the Calvinistic community spirit, Neel refuses to leave with the young man, since that action would mean betraying the faith of the pastor, a triumphant Swedenborg personality.

In "Cynthia" we are finally introduced to an Argentine background, but it is the Buenos Aires of the elegant Barrio Norte, Palermo—the local Bois de Boulogne—and the luxurious Plaza Hotel. Cynthia, the heroine, happens to be a Nordic blonde complete with a Rolls Royce who reminds us of Darío's *marquesas verlenianas*. The imagery is more dynamic in this story and the visual elements are skillfully used to underline the mental apperceptions. Such metaphors as "sprouted youth" (*adolescencia espigada*) or "foamlike chatter" (*charla espumosa*) exemplify his preoccupation with style, although such similes as "bubblylike champagne" (*expansiva como el champaña*) take us back half a century to the *premodernista* poetry of a Gutiérrez Nájera.

"Six Poems for Georgia" ("Seis poemas para Georgia") represents a fictionalized reaction to Charlie Chaplin's silent film *The Gold Rush*. Mallea imagines Georgia as forming an inextricable part of the past and present life in some Alaskan frontier town complete with the unavoidable saloon where she dances nightly. Not unlike Arabella, Georgia is described as "unemotional . . . distant . . . heartless . . . feminine" (*deshumanizada . . . inasible . . . despiadada . . . feminina*), a recurring image that will take on an added dimension in later works. Georgia looms as an inaccessible figure, Galatea-like, pondering about some abstract notion that could move her emotionally and offer an explanation for her nostalgia. She exhibits an almost metaphysical thirst to find a justification for her very existence. Although besieged by a nightly essence of maleness, she yearns for an invented hero, who even on the imagined level possesses precious little flesh and blood. Georgia's search for a *raison d'être* actually seems to parallel that of her creator.

The most developed of the stories belonging to this volume is "Confession" ("Confesión"). Here Mallea chose an interior monologue again. The protagonist, an Argentine painter who lived in France, met a woman called Malva who suffers acutely from tuberculosis. They move to London where he takes odd jobs to support them until he suddenly decides to leave. Upon returning to his native Buenos Aires he begins to relive the shared experiences and to incriminate himself for having left Malva to her fate.

Disregarding the copious references to such painters as Matisse and Derain or musicians like Eric Satie and Wanda Landowska, the salient feature of the story lies in the creation of a boundless anguish stemming from a feeling of solitude and personal failure, waxing to a note of pathos and suffering that moves the reader to genuine compassion. The stylistic treatment is also more functional than evidenced in the other stories. Similes like ". . . destiny opened my eyes as wide as one opens the door of an empty house" (". . . el destino abrió mis ojos de par en par como cuando se abren las puertas de una casa desalquilada")[22] reach an essence that is absent in the companion pieces. Mallea's obligatory theme, the inability to relate to one another and the subsequent awareness of total isolation, appear very clearly in this early piece. When writing that "not even our kisses belonged to us; we were unable to impress on our lips the flavor of passion, it felt as if we kissed each other eternally goodbye,"[23] the futility of expressing oneself through love shuts the final door to any possible pretentions to happiness. The narrator of "Confession" who nightly walks through the silent endless streets of the big city searching for an answer foreshadows the male protagonists of *The City on the Motionless River (La ciudad junto al río inmóvil)*, probably his best collection of novelettes and which appeared about eight years later.

Perhaps the most significant line in "Confession" is the opening one—mirroring Mallea's personal dilemma—in which the narrator exclaims scornfully, "My dandyish ways are being destroyed in the

fires of my misery and the boiling waters of impotence."[24] Eduardo
Mallea, the intense young man who lived a facile, dandyish existence, far removed from the toils and troubles of the majority of his
Argentine fellowmen, realized that he needed to transcend his
apparent self in order to reach a more meaningful existence. From
here on he will carry this attempt onto several intellectual and
artistic levels.

CHAPTER 2

The Formation of a Passion

I *Transitional Years*

ONE year after the publication of *Stories for a Desperate Englishwoman* Mallea began his lifelong association with the newspaper *La Nación*. In 1927 the young author decided to leave the study of law once and for all and finally confronted his father with his stand. The doctor may have been nonplussed but also realized that he could hardly deny his son's arguments concerning the importance of *La Nación* within the framework of Argentine culture, history, and politics, a trinity close to the heart of the rational thinker from San Juan. *La Nación* had been founded by the Mitre family and Dr. Mallea was an admirer of Bartolomé Mitre's poetry as well as of the Mitres' political philosophy. *La Nación's* literary supplement exemplified the pinnacle of literary taste; none other than the great poet from Nicaragua, Rubén Darío himself, had been a correspondent for the paper and in 1927 Leopoldo Lugones, the Argentine poet and author of the *Gaucho War (La guerra gaucha)*, had taken Darío's place. Eduardo Mallea soon became convinced that his father was not displeased at the prospect of seeing his younger son associated with cultural history on a level not too distant from the one he himself approached and developed during his regular literary *tertulias,* namely, that of an educated man in the classical sense who will use his best efforts to spiritualize himself by associating with the great catalytic agents of *higher* culture. Dr. Mallea wrote a letter of introduction to Luis Mitre, and young Eduardo was well received in the austerely elegant office on Florida Street. One year later Eduardo, accompanied by his parents, took a ship to Europe and carried out his first big assignment: to cover the Olympic games held in Amsterdam in 1928.

31

His recollections of this trip found their way into such novels as *European Nocturne (Nocturno europeo), The Bay of Silence (La bahía de silencio),* and *The Rembrandts (Los Rembrandt),* but only after the initial exposure to the European reality had become assimilated and reworked over a number of years. Mallea apparently was subconsciously aware of the need to fulfill his apprenticeship, primarily an initiation into the nature and mold of what to him seemed to be the sum total of Europe's heritage—and which would in some way be used later to shape and complement his Argentine experience and legacy. Certainly the proud admirer of his *criollo* forefathers and the spirit of the pampas showed himself to be a most willing and impressionable student of what the old Continent had to offer to his eyes and ears. From 1927 to 1934 this most prolific of prose writers in later life did not complete a single manuscript.

In 1934 he returned to Europe, now as editor of *La Nación*'s Sunday "Literary Supplement," perhaps the most prestigious position in the world of Argentine letters. He had been invited to give some lectures in Italy and also to stay at Victoria Ocampo's home in Paris. Victoria Ocampo was a descendant of Argentina's foremost landed gentry and possessed a spirit of independence and self-reliance that today could easily be associated with the stand of the liberated woman but which was rare in the context of Latin American norms of behavior of the 1930s. She had decided to use some of her inheritance to found and maintain a literary magazine dedicated to the arts, letters, and music in the grand style of the cosmopolitan European journals. The name of the magazine was *Sur,* and from 1931 to 1969 *Sur* became the focus of the cosmopolitan-minded Argentine writers, artists, and musicians, backed by Victoria Ocampo's financial contribution, a feat that earned her the animosity of the militant left as well as the ultranationalistic right. While Eduardo Mallea was speaking in Rome and Milan, Victoria Ocampo held her talks in Florence and Como.[1]

A good number of impressions from his European journey are reflected in *European Nocturne* and *The Bay of Silence,* the latter perhaps his most significant novel. He met a number of outstanding members of the European intelligentsia: Paul Valéry and Jean Giraudoux in Paris, Nicholas Berdyaev and Alberto Moravia in Pontigny, and Luigi Pirandello in Rome. By his own admission Mallea was not only quite dazzled by the presence of these luminaries, but he also found inspiration to continue their aesthetic and spiritual contributions in what he termed "a story of passion, faith, vitality, and need for grandeur that led him to overcome his literary inactivity in order to enter into his particular brand of testimonial."[2] Decades later when he was prompted by an aging Victoria Ocampo to recall the, most intense and meaningful highlights of this European experience for a volume entitled *Dialogue with Mallea* *(Diálogo con Mallea)*, he mentioned his meetings with the poet Paul Valéry at the latter's club on the Champs Elysées, his conversations with Drieu de la Rochelle, the French nationalist with whom he had long discussions about Faulkner and Nietzsche, and the inspiring presence of André Breton, whose surrealist manifestoes had changed the style of many writers. Being next to greatness certainly had been a tradition Mallea acquired from his father, and the young author reacted with proper and conditioned enthusiasm to the stimulus of the Old World's culture. He later acknowledged that this experience had prompted him to contrast the European mode with his native one.[3] Even though this comparison was carried out on a largely subconscious level, the confrontation of the European essence with the Argentine spirit resulted in a special awareness concerning his own heritage and destiny. Having largely overcome his *modernista* tendencies, overtly visible in *Stories for a Desperate Englishwoman*, Mallea in 1934 could react to the lure of Europe by looking back to his homeland from a European-based perspective that carried the advantage of distance and detachment.

II   Knowledge and Expression of Argentina

His gestation period drawing to a close, Mallea came out in 1935 with *Knowledge and Expression of Argentina (Conocimiento y expresión de la Argentina)*, a slender volume based on the lecture he gave the previous year in the Palacio Giustiniano of Rome as well as in the Millione Gallery in Milan. Although written in essay form and addressed to a European audience, Mallea was able to fashion a dialogue with himself that centered around a New World imagination and, in a way, laid the foundation for later pronouncements on personal and national quests for salvation. After an initial tribute to Dante, Pascal, and Valéry, an ascending order of Europe's most treasured intellects, Mallea turns inward and presents himself as a simple *homo americanus* whose "American truth" arises from an "American drama of humanity" that binds the people of the New World together in a dramatic plight of universal proportions.

As Mallea goes on to define this plight, his arguments become rather ontological, and the focus is centered on his homeland. He begins to develop the collective persona of the new Adam in-the-making, one who finds himself at the stage of being shaped by the national forces of the American soil. This new Adam, then, stands at the crossroads, looking forward to a chance for a personal and collective self-expression that lies somewhere in the distance but realizing that the road to fulfillment is not quite discernible. Mallea tries to find a corresponding terminology that would allow him to verbalize this rather anguished American condition. His Americans listen to the voices of the fields and prairies, gestating "an inarticulate cry in their silence."[4] At the same time they reject "the crude and automatic way of life of the United States" because they are compelled to seek a genuine transcendental knowledge that is an outgrowth of the Edenic fields of the new continent. And only thus, Mallea reasons, "their history would be that of a passion";[5] for it is based on a "knowledge and expression of our essence."[6]

But Mallea does not dwell too long on the American destiny. Rather, he turns to examining the physical boundaries of Argentina, from Tierra del Fuego to the Chaco jungle, and then makes a rapid excursion to its confines by traveling through arid lands and vast fertile plains before retreating to the focal point, so obligatory for most Argentine writers, that of the metropolitan capital. From this fixed position he adopts a historical perspective that allows him to evaluate cultural and organic elements that have shaped the all-too-brief genesis of *argentinidad*. In this task, however, his position or premises are far from clear. He pays tribute to the gaucho, "the country dweller whose emotional mode is both deeply and nobly felt"[7] and who constitutes the prototype of the Argentine man born at the turn of the century. From this point onward Mallea blends the historical course of Argentina with his personal one, thus synchronizing the two destinies. By the same token, the man from the turn of the century who now pounds the asphalt-covered streets and sidewalks of the city on the motionless river enacts his daily odyssey in search of the invisible and dormant Argentina. Cut off from the land and isolated from other human beings, the big-city Argentine Adam will, according to Mallea, suffer in silence, as he cannot overcome the alienation of modern urban existence or bring any other meaning into his daily life. At the same time, the fertile land makes its riches available to feed the city and insures its well-being, a process that only helps to expand the institutions that proliferate as accomplices of the greed and materialism that hold sway over the urban spirit. The man from the turn of the century—akin to the author—will reject all cultural models that represent the falsification of life and will instead search for kindred souls and try to establish a subterranean affinity with the spirit of the land, the invisible Argentina: "Look, then, at this man who is seeking like a lost lover, throughout an endless night of evil and uncertainty, the nourishment for his hunger . . . his yearning for a creation of a harmonious order and the original language of a New World coming upward from the roots."[8]

Mallea senses and envisions the existence of such a man, part of his own generation, who might be a politician, an artist, or simply someone with enough sensitivity to look for a more meaningful future. These men are as yet not united but exist as independent cells submerged in the multiplicity of the Argentinian Babylon—Buenos Aires. As they emerge they are sure to surpress and eventually eliminate the contamination imposed upon them by the city and its nonspiritual life. For Mallea, these chosen people constitute an elite charged with a definite mission: "the history of these men will be the history of the progress of a conscience."[9] Nothing less will do.

It would, of course, be easy to question aspects of this essay by simply asking for more precise definitions concerning such concepts as "spiritual consciousness," "the hidden and potential life," or the meaning of "political mysticism." It is equally possible to be puzzled by equations like "the city is a sea of empty words" or formulations like "these young men do possess a mental vocation that is fervidly militant."

No doubt the reader is faced with a volatile spirit, a somewhat amorphous dosage of personal ethics and a personalized fervor that stems from Mallea's attempt to find the collective soul of his *argentinidad* and to discover this condition in those who are deemed worthy to embody it. But in essence he is struggling here with an ontological problem that can yield a double conclusion: to discover the genuine self and to find the true collective spirit of his people. That is why Mallea wants to tear off masks, uncover the layers of false urban civilization and put his ear on the ground of the silent pampas in order to listen for the heartbeat of the land. Moving between such focal points as the romantics' search for the origin of a collective spirit and Max Scheler's concept of the true persona,

Mallea manages to communicate a basic quest, namely to search in all earnestness for a meaningful existence within a national framework with the help of the literary and philosophical arsenal furnished by the past, a European past. This is a large order, and it hardly surprises us that Mallea is not successful in solving the problems connected with the implementation of this quest. To a large extent, this impasse explains why he continues to belabor this dual ontological problem. In fact, he will soon begin to take the themes and subthemes stated in this essay and fictionalize them in a number of works, a practice that earned him the criticism in some quarters of producing fictionalized and repetitious essays. At any rate, *Knowledge and Expression of Argentina* foreshadows works like *The City on the Motionless River* and *The Bay of Silence* that contain some of his finest writing.

III   European Nocturne

Mallea's next work, *European Nocturne*, also reflects the trip to France and Italy in 1934. Although of novel length, the volume can hardly be considered novelistic, since it projects largely impressions of a voyage or reflections on local phenomena that are usually found in a diary. Adrian, the narrator and sole main character, moves in and out of venerable *pallazzi* and art galleries; he peers at classical landscapes and remnants of antiquity; and he never ceases to analyze his relationship to a Europe weighed down by its own heritage and old age.

But in spite of the static mode Mallea has managed to inject several levels of awareness that flow in parallel waves through this nocturne. The first of these levels corresponds to the theme of regeneration, found already in *Knowledge and Expression of Argentina*, a theme that manifests itself through the social interaction of Adrian in the sterile world of hotels, resorts, and tourist attractions. The second level comprises an Argentine-European confrontation that must have been akin to Mallea's own emotional reaction when Adrian stands in front of Leonardo de Vinci's David, conscious of the lifeless, flat pampas imbedded deeply inside of his memory. The third level, though tenuous and sketchy, deals with the sociopolitical realities of Europe in the 1930s, a decade that served as theater for ideological clashes that would soon turn into the grimmest of exercises in death, suffering, and destruction, beginning with the tragic civil war in Spain in 1936.

On the first or personal level Mallea quotes Gertrude Stein's remark supposedly made to Ernest Hemingway in the Paris of the American expatriots during the Roaring Twenties: "You are the lost generation." The connection to Adrian's European wanderings is obvious. He too has left the New World to search for a meaning to life that was not revealed to him in his own culture. Yet, neither pilgrimage ended in a restoration of faith or the solving of existential quests. The reader finds Adrian wistfully staring at the Seine River near the Ile de la Cité and feeling an ill wind that is blowing the seeds of tragic dissolution; he feels a sense of fury that changes into one of hopelessness: ". . . he felt alone; absolutely alone. His misery was boundless. He looked everywhere for a human being that would offer him a possibility of communing."[10]

In his daily search for a meaningful interchange Adrian walks along the Parisian boulevards from Raspail to the Saint Michel, dropping in and out of bistros, cafés and restaurants, the obligatory milieu of Mallea himself. Adrian's sadness is absolute; in fact, it even determines his conception of the female element. He becomes intrigued by a woman whose Slavic features and air of sensuousness remind him curiously enough of a figure in the Parthenon. But when he finally manages to exchange some words with her she impresses him as being "violent and virile." A more significant relationship develops when he meets Miss Dardington, a woman of thirty-two from Virginia who seems to have come out of *Stories for a Desperate Englishwoman*. She is grey-eyed, slender, long-legged, aristocratic, aloof, and cocksure of herself. Adrian reacts more positively to this figure, although initially he sums her up as "a woman with predatory eyes, lips, and gestures, always ready to trap something."[11] In later scenes their meetings are at least tinted with an incipient sensual desire if not passion on his part. If Adrian's "communion" with Ira Dardington fails to reach even the most elementary levels of carnal passion it is due to the fact that the main character is not capable of allowing himself a libidinal release. The style certainly underlines this mental attitude. Adrian, the determined autoanalyst, sees his double sitting in front of the cool and autocratic Ira and sternly pronounces judgment on the other Adrian, baiting him for reacting with animalistic impulses, "with epidermic emotions" manipulated by his glandular secretion in a most ignoble exhibition.[12] Earlier in the novel Adrian had exhibited a similar reaction against his "baser nature" when he attended a music-hall

show at the Bal Tabarin in Paris and had cast some aroused glances
at the generous display of "female meat" (viandas exhibidas), to
quote Mallea's strangely archaic and puritanical choice of imagery.[13]

But once the drawing-room scene with Ira Dardington has been
carried to an ambiguous ending, Adrian is free to revert to his
natural self that finds an emotional outlet by roaming once more the
grey and deserted streets of Paris, an occupation that Mallea ascribes to his protagonists in later works.

Adrian's alienation accompanies him to Italy where the milieu is
an exact duplication of the one he found in Paris, namely, the world
of hotels, bars, and restaurants filled by the inevitable burgeois elite
that dominated this peculiar scene in the 1930s, before the advent
of mass tourism and the age of the common man. This moneyed
group, however, brought no spiritual or aesthetic values to
truthseekers like Adrian. Surrounded by tuxedoes, evening gowns,
and oversolicitous headwaiters Adrian silently sits, eats, drinks, and
stares, saturated with ennui and emptiness.[14] The last two nouns are
repeated throughout the work as the same supporting cast sur-
rounds the protagonist in France and Italy.

Toward the end of the novel Adrian expands his social interaction;
however, it becomes the basis for an apocalyptic vision that encompasses an enormous multitude whose "dark voices galloping across
the Earth" pollute the cities.[15] For Adrian a collective spiritualization was needed to elevate the multitude's way of life to a level of
meaningful existence. He felt strongly that his own misery was also
an interlude to a higher stage and saw his salvation made feasible
through the very act of loving, of giving freely of himself, of becoming a "man-river" (río-hombre) who would be irresistibly drawn
toward a natural order of humanity.[16] But his theorizing ceases as he
falls back again on the sterility of his upper-class milieu, his sole
certainty being the impression of the Arno river flowing darkly
under a somber September sky. Walled off from life Adrian desper-
ately yearns for an organic state that would allow him to forego his
cerebral state and intellectual barrenness. Thus he dreams of a life
rhythm akin to that of clouds, water, and trees: "If one could only
impose on one's life the rhythm of the clouds . . . the waters
. . . the trees . . .";[17] but, once again, he is not able to transform his
yearnings into a workable philosophy of life.

On the second level Mallea takes his protagonist to "open his
lungs to the European air."[18] The Old World offers the visitor from

the pampas and the urbanized shores of the River Plate multiple forms of history and tradition in the guise of ancient sites and monuments, cathedrals and palaces, art galleries and opera houses. Adrian visits the old market squares lined with Baroque facades in Brugge, Amsterdam, and Brussels; he admires the frescoes at the Medici-Riccardi palace in Florence; he is reminded of Ariosto, Voltaire, and Botticelli and reflects on the merits of Michelangelo's David as well as Gian Bellini's Sacred Allegories; the spirit of Machiavelli seems to emmanate from the Ponte Vecchio over the Arno river and the age of the Quattrocento lingers on in the corners of the *plazoletta* in Venice. Adrian reacts to Europe with the reverential mood that stems from a deep knowledge and a prolonged mental association conerning a favorite subject. For Adrian—as for the author—the European experience has been conditioned by evocations and a sort of *Bildungserlebnis*, a formative experience, fashioned at the *tertulias* and *soirées* held by the Argentine elite that actually constituted Sarmiento's cadres in charge of Europeanizing Argentina. It was this cultural indoctrination that placed so many of Mallea's compatriots in a position halfway across the Atlantic in search for a past that had eluded them. For the critic José Bianco, Adrian-Mallea responds deeply to an old established order and an enduring tradition that are reworked in the mind of the present. "[Adrian] understands that the Europeans don't have to learn or acquire anything. They would only need to remember. . . . And Adrian looks at Europe with sorrowful eyes, a little childish perhaps, full of hope—New World eyes, adequate enough, for the times, to capture Europe's secrets."[19]

On the third level Adrian's emotional self remains alien to the European reality; in fact, he cannot become absorbed by the giant ground swell of conflicting ideologies, social struggles, or military confrontation in the making. Only temporarily does Adrian register an awareness of the "Spirit of the Thirties" and the "Gathering Storm" over Paris, Berlin, London, and Rome. Early in the novel the impending war is viewed within the context of an order menaced by erupting, chaotic forces, the sad by-products of an all too human condition. In a most Spenglerian mood Adrian is convinced that the post-Renaissance era with its antispiritual evolution, aggravated by the rise of materialistic ambition, extreme capitalistic practices, and the rise of nationalism, would lead to the destruction of an order that was barely able to survive the erosion of World War

I.[20] It was a matter of "Europe not being able to control its strange neurosis"[21] and drifting into a cataclysmic maelstrom that manifested itself to Adrian through occasional references to Marx and Engels, Lenin and Stalin, or some workers in Fiesole noisily celebrating the Bolshevik October Revolution.

Clearly a marginal figure, Adrian can neither participate in the spirit of the social upheaval nor can he consciously belong to the bourgeois world of the man and woman who parade their evening clothes as a class symbol. Thus his marginality becomes transformed into tedium and alienation. The apparent remedy for his uncommitted state is to be consumed by a spiritual purification that would somehow be accomplished by giving of himself, of becoming the *río-hombre*, a human flow that overcomes the obstacles of erected self-interest and sterile hermeticism. Certainly the compulsion to transcend his bourgeois limitations and cerebral self-analysis comes through as the major preoccupation in the work.

Upon his return to Argentina Mallea delivered a lecture in the city of Rosario entitled "The Present-Day Writer Looks at His Time" ("El escritor de hoy frente a su tiempo"), that subsequently appeared in *Sur*[22] and in which the concept of transcendence becomes further developed. For the critic José Bianco this essay provides a clear portrayal of Mallea's indebtedness to the philosophy of Nicholas Berdyaev. Like the Russian, Mallea proposes to overcome the imperfect and temporary condition of the human being by relying on the sheer force of spiritualized love. Only Mallea goes one step further than Berdyaev upon demanding a love-force arising out of an act of total self-sacrifice.[23]

IV   The City on the Motionless River

In 1963 Mallea stated in his autobiographical reminiscences called *The Inner War (La guerra interior)* that he had written most of *European Nocturne* on a ship returning to Argentina; he further claimed an inspiration from a vision of the Old World in its twilight stage.[24] But he also stated that he was already looking ahead toward a second confrontation, namely, that of the writer who must reinterpret his personal and cultural tenets in the light of newly acquired impressions and experiences. This confrontation led to the formulation of his *History of an Argentine Passion* that appeared in 1938.

Another important volume, however, preceded his *History*. Between 1931 and 1935 Mallea had written a number of *nouvelles* and stories that were now put together under the title *The City on the Motionless River*. Three of the pieces included in this volume had been published previously, which throws a new light on his long period of gestation between *Stories for a Desperate Englishwoman* and *European Nocturne*.[25] "Submersion" ("Sumersión") came out in *Sur* and "The Lost Cause of Jacob Uber" ("La causa de Jacobo Uber, perdida") as well as "Anguish" ("Angustia") appeared in Spain's *Revista de Occidente*. Mallea could hardly have found more prestigious outlets in the whole Spanish-speaking world.

For the attentive reader of *European Nocturne* many of the men and women who populate the city on the motionless river are strongly reminiscent of Adrian in that they act like marginal beings, striving for a nexus with what Mallea himself called "the great sum of human awareness."[26]

Several critics have summed up the *nouvelles* as examples of existentialist tendencies, featuring a number of solitary beings who move around quite aimlessly in their own labyrinth of anguish and alienation.[27] As a spiritual geographer Mallea does indeed pay continued attention to one of his main gravitational points: the huge Argentine metropolis with its built-in anonymity that creates its own type of emptiness in the midst of the multitude rushing back and forth in its daily activities, a movement dictated by an artificial way of life bereft of spiritual meaning. City life actually plays a dominant role in much of Mallea's fiction, whether the setting is Paris, Amsterdam, or the habitually prominent Argentine capital. Silvina Bullrich, Argentina's most successful contemporary novelist, who in her own way has produced the most outstanding portrayals of the urbanized Argentine upper middle class, found in *The City on the Motionless River* an urban essence that she could share, a city she loved in spite of "the cold indifference of its inhabitants . . . a city avidly seeking leisure and ostentatiousness, and where vanity and egotism motivate and contaminate each person."[28] Some of her best novels, including *Los burgueses*, which deals with the decadence of a patrician family, and *Los salvadores de la patria (The Saviors of the Country)*, a satire on political and military intrigues in the capital, constitute a realistic counterpart to Mallea's portrayal. Mallea's own vision of the Argentine *homo urbanus* shows a deep concern with the negative aspects cited by Silvina Bullrich. In the introduction to *The City on the Motionless River* he tells about the need to unearth "the subterranean man of America" whose isolation and silence must be led to bring forth a humanistic cry.[29] This need must of course be implemented, and here the complexities of modern urban life create an almost overwhelming task. Thus it is not surprising that the author's scheme of things encompasses not only an ontological concern but also a social, historical, and even political level. The "humanistic cry," however, appears to be as elusive as the concretion of the genuine spirit of *argentinidad* that in Mallea's eyes will be reborn or recaptured through the process of breaking the hermetic bonds of the artificial city life.

Here some very old themes are being recast and reinterpreted by the young writer who had come from the provincial Bahía Blanca, filled with reminiscences of his father's *Zeitgeist*, to the Babylon on the River Plate. The author's Argentina seems rooted in a humanistic morality that goes back to the thoughts of Juan Bautista Alberdi and Domingo Faustino Sarmiento, true representatives of the Argentine enlightenment in its formative era during the nineteenth century. Both of those men fashioned the sociopolitical outlook of Dr. Mallea as he practiced medicine in the small towns besieged by the endless and primitive pampas. Eduardo Mallea absorbed this humanistic legacy of European thought and projected it, consciously as well as subconsciously, onto the contemporary Argentine social scene.

A paradoxical situation developed only when he insisted on the search for an Argentine essence within the beings that populate the Parisianlike boulevards and streets of Buenos Aires, an essence rising from a uniquely fashioned New World inspiration. Perhaps Salvador de Madariaga's definition of humanism helps to reconcile Mallea's divergent position. For the Spanish essayist humanism represents the generalization of individualism, an attitude that adopts not a fixed moral, social, or technical point of view but rather a position that integrates arts and sciences in one indivisible fabric. Madariaga's Spaniard, defined as a "man of passion," will not surrender his totality to any given outlook, discipline, or activity. Rather, he would feel free to create an enlarged self that would hopefully strive to attain a level of inner nobility, a theme always close to the core of Hispanic thinking from Cervantes to Ortega y Gasset. In his quest to uncover the Argentine Adam, uncontaminated by the sons of his European forefathers, Mallea puts the alliance between European humanism and the New World spirit on a most precarious basis. Yet in doing so, he joins a number of American writers who took the almost original land to belong to the New World's Garden of Eden, tailor-made to serve as the purifying instrument for the Chosen People whose wisdom of Paradise Regained would impel them to become spiritualized enough to knock at the gates of heaven. Here Mallea stands very much on the side of such influential Argentine writers as Juan Bautista Alberdi, Manuel Gálvez, and Ezequiel Martínez Estrada, the latter two outstanding contemporaries.

Although Mallea often writes in terms of the *homo americanus* in search of purification and spiritualization his fictional beings are usually Argentine. José Bianco focuses on Mallea's concern for the perfectability of the Argentine national character in what he considers to be the works of his most promising period—and which include *The City on the Motionless River, History of an Argentine Passion,* and *The Bay of Silence:* "There exists in the Argentine a spiritual 'I' capable of harnessing an intense emotional richness . . . and to elevate his passions and give them a worthy goal . . . filled with what Mallea calls 'the authentic greatness of our own race' . . . and in which resides the 'essential basis of the Argentine.' "[30]

Without considering at this point the question of a nationalistic awareness, it becomes nevertheless clear that the city, with its steel and concrete, gas fumes, neon lights, and traffic jams, is hardly conducive to creating an awareness on the part of the modern inhabitant concerning the purifying forces of the land, Mallea's "ethical land." Yet, Mallea's predilection for the urban setting and the sensitive, educated men and women who incessantly wander through the asphalt maze, was born out of an affinity for this urban rhythm, thus forcing him to search for the deep and spiritual Argentina while pounding the endless sidewalks and streets that choke the earth. At the end of the introduction to *The City on the Motionless River* Mallea touchingly takes the reader by the hand exclaiming: "Let's go to the city," his ever present city.

Of all the *nouvelles* making up this volume "Submersion" serves as the most dramatic introduction to Mallea's urban labyrinth. The sole protagonist, a European, perhaps a Greek, by the name of Avesquin leaves his ship eager to explore the New World and to interact with its people. What follows, however, is a nightmarish experience that ends with Avesquin fleeing back to the port in order to take the next ship, presumably to carry him back across the Atlantic. The author has the reader accompany Avesquin past the immigrants' barracks where several thousand wait each week to be allowed into the Promised Land. Beyond the drawbridges and the docks the immense port district shows its grey, impersonal, and at times hostile mask, divided into a "thousand diagonals made of white cement," filled with the shrill voices of hydraulic hammers, whistles, and shouts, and populated by tired and wan men and women, each one an island, an enigma, wrapped in "brutal silence." After a stay of two weeks Avesquin begins to develop an "unspeakable hatred for this populated and organized desert" where an endless maze only serves to convey strange people to a lonely destiny. Staying at a nondescript port hotel, keeping himself in the silence of his narrow room, and floating aimlessly along the streets where everyone hurries along wrapped in his secret self, Avesquin begins to experience a monumental anguish. "He now was suffering a monumental torture, not only due to his complete isolation but also his yearning for the fresh fountains of life, the earth, for what is not burned under the crust of sterility. The asphalt surface filled him with a sordid helplessness."[31]

Rejecting the artificiality of the "false symbols and the hallucinations" Avesquin evokes the vision of another Argentina, one abounding in "fertile lands, pampas, vineyards, and mountains"; and he envisions the life-giving archetypal symbols that nourish his anguished imagination: sun, light, rain, earth, and human joy.

Avesquin's decisive defeat occurs in his repeated attempts to establish meaningful human relationships. He frequents the bars and cafés of the port district only to find another level of artificiality, the feigned interest of the prostitutes, "the painted sirens who prey upon Ulysses' crew" in the darkish and damp hovels around the docks in a peculair kind of Hades that even stirred the imagination of Mallea's contemporary Jorge Luis Borges and prompted him to write poems like *Paseo de Julio*, reflecting a sordid and private hell. But Avesquin's climactic confrontation with Buenos Aires does not happen here. By chance he meets a girl in a shabby movie theater and attempts to establish a dialogue. While his failure is due to a poor command of Spanish, hers resides in an absolute inability to express her feelings and react to his humanity. The mutual failure to understand each other's inner needs are aggravated by a desperate attempt on the part of Avesquin to succeed on the physical level. The girl does visit his shabby hotel room but fails to respond to his human warmth. "Touch me if you want to," she tells him with severity "but don't try to kiss me." When he makes a gesture to embrace her, she pushes him away, only to undress with grave and sad movements carefully folding her clothes on a chair: "Hers was a new and beautiful flesh, harsh and inviolate like the city, flesh filled with silence, strong and firm, amid the humid shadows, no longer embodying the European earth."[32]

But her docility involves an abjectness that manifests itself as a "docile and repulsive abandonment" for Avesquin who is struck by the empty gestures arising out of a passivity that eliminates all personal involvement. Avesquin abruptly leaves his room and flees through the deserted streets, past the vagabonds sleeping on the park benches, down to the silent docks in the cold of the night. Only upon reaching the ships does a feeling of relief creep into his consciousness. He will await the new day here, already distant from the desert of stone and cement that is called Buenos Aires.

Throughout the story Mallea employs a descriptive technique that establishes the city as a monstrous organism that molds the minds and emotions of its victims to the point of dehumanization: "bundles of people with the look of docile beasts," submerged in a "pitiless Babylon" and filled with "brutal deafness." But Mallea's determinism is not that of the literary naturalists who, like the early Gálvez in *Nacha Regules* (1919), were still publishing works in the 1930s. Rather, Mallea offers the reader a Kafka-like confrontation between the individual and an impersonal, all-pervasive entity that claims the mass-man and creates a deep feeling of anguish in those who, like Avesquin, are bearers of sensitivity and intelligence.

The second story, "Solves or Immaturity," ("Solves o la Inmadurez") features two of Mallea's favorite characters: the aristocratic and self-assured female and the undecided, searching male, almost a Hamlet-figure, who is forever questioning his motivations, urges, and purpose in life. Cristiana Ruiz and Juan Sebastián Solves have been living together for over six months in her luxury apartment in downtown Buenos Aires near the Retiro area where the elegant Barrio Norte begins. Both are highly talented and educated people with an enormous artistic as well as human potential. Cristiana, a stage designer, has studied at Yale and in Paris. She is presently involved in the stage production of Ibsen's *Hedda Gabler;* and she has, perhaps, more than a professional interest in the heroine of this play, since both are depicted as "strong-willed, cold, intelligent, domineering." Next to her, Solves appears as vacillating, aimless, and weak. Yet, there is an inner self active in him that grows almost independently and finally overshadows his relationship with Cristiana. Time and again, the two protagonists are placed in an obvious juxtaposition: "She facing life by perennially demanding and violently dictating her wishes" while he allowed himself to be "guided, astonished, beguiled, and deceived by these life forces."[33] Solves slowly begins to realize that he is really wrapped within himself—*ensimismado*—ruminating unclear thoughts and listening for an inaudible rhythm of the land. "I am like the wind that blows over the land," he tells Cristiana[34] who, assured and systematic, goes about her daily routine knowing exactly what she wants. Like his creator, Solves is a literary man; however, this state does not seem to afford him a meaningful goal. His introspection and intuitive action take him away from any methodical pursuit or analysis; and he is only aware of some inarticulate forces in him that seem to be tied to the dual voices coming from the land. Mallea attempts to define these forces, yet he is only able to formulate a vague approximation and then through Cristiana's reflections:

She had never seen a man who resembled his land as much as Solves: he showed this indefinite yet profound quality that is inherent in the pampas, boundless and fleeting. His whole being was fluid like the land without frontiers; sad, monotonous, wandering from emotion to emotion, yet without giving himself to anything, as if searching for something that would be his someday in some form.[35]

At times Solves appears to take on a populist stance, talking with exultation about an American humanity on the move and quoting Whitman: "Solitary, singing in the West, I strike for a New World . . . ;"[36] but his basic preoccupation points to an ontological quest. He feels the need to mature in a state of solitude, vigilance, and suffering in order to know what he is or what he is meant to be. Although the story ends inconclusively, Solves is limited to the anonymous beings who, like he, "walk through the nocturnal city in search of their submerged realities."[37] Here Mallea can finally make a transition onto a national level exclaiming "Oh, Argentines, people filled with slow, concentrated emotions, emotions not yet verbalized, supressed, vehement, taciturn, striving to emerge from the deep center of each being."[38]

In the next story, "The Rhapsody of the Merry Culprit" ("La rapsodia del alegre malhechor"), the protagonist represents the negation of the qualities that are so dear to Mallea. Carlos Oro arrives by train in Buenos Aires after having spent two years in a faraway provincial town, and in ecstatic anticipation of intense experiences that would satisfy his starved senses. Oro's sensatory craving is so great that he can hardly wait for the train to come to a final halt; and he is eager to swallow the city, its streets, shops, cafés, bars, men, and women with an almost metaphysical determination. Impetuous and dynamic, he is determined to distill every minute of his stay into a hedonistic essence, thus failing to see the city's characteristics as described by the author: "a monstrous and grey city, passively spread out for him like a giant harlot."[39] In his exuberant state Carlos Oro rushes from one end of the city to another, bathing in the multitude of people in the shopping streets: Florida, Santa Fe, Avenida de Mayo. He feels the need to talk to the shopkeepers, he cannot let a pretty female go by without murmuring a phrase of admiration into her ear. His path quickens as he makes contact with old companions and former girl friends, but the encounters only last until the novelty has worn off. His compulsion makes him "use up" people and places, giddily rushing onward to meet new sensations and situations.

Oro remains unaware of the inner struggles, the problems, sorrows, or expectations of others. Oblivious to all but his self-expression and gratification, he fails to realize that the economic depression has ruined his friends. He throws some coins to a beggar, buys expensive ties from a surprised store clerk, and shouts a hearty farewell to his impoverished friends and rushes off to a suburb where the daughter of a German watchmaker receives him with the love and affection he is still taking for granted. At a dinner party given in his honor he tells a lengthy anecdote about an Indian girl who is sexually abused by some male adventurers because she has become hypnotized by a giant flashlight that simulates the sun. A telephone call makes him return to the suburb of Belgrano where the German girl has suffered an accident. He dismisses her anguish and leaves with a cliché on his lips. He cannot endure staying at her bedside knowing that outside life is waiting. The *nouvelle* ends with

Oro running through the night in his desperate attempt not to exhaust its possibilities.

As the title indicates, the protagonist exemplifies the triumph of negative life forces. To act blindly, almost instinctively, is not compatible with what Mallea would uphold as a moral or spiritual position that ought to constitute the core of one's relationship to others. Action per se, then, can be self-defeating; and, once again, action should be guided by an agonizing search within oneself in order to find the level at which self-sacrifice and compassion can lead to a true communion with mankind. The next story, "Conversation" ("Conversación") also presents negative aspects in the protagonists. The nameless couple that spends countless hours in cafés or restaurants acting out of ennui and aimlessness exemplifies the futility of living a daily routine bereft of any values that might transcend their bourgeois condition. As usual, Mallea's main characters belong to the Argentine upper-middle class and as such can afford to spend much of their time and efforts pondering about themselves, preferably in bars, cafés, or restaurants, the author's favorite hunting grounds. "He" and "She" are in one of the downtown *bistros*, drinking, smoking, and making small talk in order to simply kill time, vainly trying to rise to a level of meaningfulness. Neither their own lives nor those of their friends and acquaintances escape a depressing and drab mediocrity. Like the characters in Ionèsco's *The Bald Soprano*, they are all interchangeable, examples of an antiheroic age in which the individual, submerged in his mass society, has long ago lost the ability of discovering the marvellous or to be moved by the spirit of the tragic that would individualize his destiny. Mallea's urban society is dominated by antiheroes whose mechanistic behavior is echoed a thousandfold by the faceless men and women who sit in similar cafés or living rooms. Their plight is not so much grounded in anguish as in a feeling of futility as they realize that it matters little what they do or refrain from doing. Mallea here cultivates a genuinely existentialist problem as he has his characters caught in a web of indecision and inaction. As "He" and "She" are debating whether to eat at a restaurant or not, whether to go home or stay at the bistro, the key line of the story takes place: "If only one could discover some purpose to life."[40]

Here Mallea returns to the question of man's uprootedness in modern society, a theme that has antecedents in the European novel of the early twentieth century. Professor John R. Polt, for instance, points out the parallels existing between Mallea's marginal beings that wander aimlessly through the *porteño* labyrinth and the characters in Maurice Barrès' novels *The Uprooted (Les Déracinès)* as well as *Berenice's Garden (Le Jardin de Bérénice)*, because both authors take up the problems of a personal fulfillment that seems inextricably tied to a national destiny. To quote Polt, "the dedication of self to an ideal in communion with and service to the authentic nation would lead to the spirit of *argentinidad.*"[41] This is not to imply that Mallea cultivates a Barrèsian type of nationalism. It becomes clear, however, that Mallea is creating a national context in order to allow his "existentialist" characters to find a certainty that would conceivably lead to a life goal, a fulfillment. Quite clearly, then, the anguish of the major characters in *The City on the Motionless River* does not stem from a loss of belief in a moral or theological system—a dilemma facing followers of the French school of existentialism such as Jean Paul Sartre—but rather is caused by a negative state of cultural awareness.

The protagonists of the remaining stories express an equally strong need to find this spiritual salvation. Ana Borel in "Anguish" ("Angustia") is another solitary being who cannot break down her own barriers erected by suspicion and fear. Her marriage to one Benes, an old friend of her father, fails to alleviate her solitude and final agony. She becomes ill and dies, aware that her life has been absolutely useless.

"The Lost Cause of Jacob Uber" ("La causa de Jacobo Uber, perdida") features one more protagonist who shows a desperate desire to establish meaningful relationships with another human being. Living in the private, humble world of an obscure desk clerk he has become accustomed to creating his own images of those around him. When he meets Carlota, a quite unattractive language teacher, he proceeds to refashion her in his imagination until the mental vision replaces the real image. As José Bianco observed, Jacobo Uber cannot transcend himself and thus must make use of the mirror image that will reflect a reality projected by him. But when the resemblance of the physical pleasure experienced with Carlota interferes with the created image, he begins to fall apart.[42] His only solution is to drown in the muddy and brackish waters of the motionless river next to the big city as he feels unable to direct his emotions to a real living being in a normal manner.

The last story to be considered is entitled "Serena Barcos." A strong-willed feminist, standing conspicuously alone in the Latin man's world of the 1930s, Serena has become disillusioned with men to the point of confessing to a woman friend that she found men to be "uninhabited sexual organisms" to whom a significant relating would seem impossible. Intelligent, resourceful, and energetic, she must find an outlet for her life forces, and she channels her passion toward a sociopolitical level on which she will pursue the dream of a utopian society in which a better social structure would insure justice for all.

In varying degrees, Solves, Cristiana, the nameless couple in "Conversation," Ana Borel, Jacob Uber, and Serena Barcos make a case for the author's quest, that of the need to dedicate oneself to something higher and greater than one's limited "present self."[43] All of these protagonists share a common background: they are sensitive, educated, intelligent, urbanized, and like Adrian in *European Nocturne,* they are lonely, unfulfilled entities walking the silent streets of the large, nocturnal city. But since their creator cannot specify a prescribed remedy or solution that would embody a personal as well as collective salvation, the protagonists can at best look forward to a state of *becoming* as they try to transcend their self-contained world.

V   History of an Argentine Passion

The late Luis Emilio Soto once defined *History of an Argentine Passion* as Mallea's intellectual disintoxication. The author himself referred to this book as a "cry of enamored dust, vehement, emotional, linked to my country in life and death."[44] It is not surprising that such poetic ardor is accompanied by an admission that the work was written in a feverish hurry, as if afraid to examine his flow of words with sober rationality. Mallea could afford to criticize his candor as well as the hurried style, since he placed himself in the role of the prodigal son who returned from his European experience only to fall in love with his native soil. Such a role had advantages since it allowed for a confessional made of expression that needed little if any validation and which could rely on self-realization rather than documentation.

Structurally, *History of an Argentine Passion* shows eleven divisions and a preface. The latter constitutes an exulted plea to the submerged Argentine who is in grave danger of losing his national essence unless he can awaken to his civic responsibilities and begin making use of intellectual and emotive resources for the benefit of a national destiny.[45] In the first two divisions Mallea traces his own genesis: the childhood years in the sea port of Bahía Blanca, family life, the English grammar school, the lure of the Atlantic, the family's move to Buenos Aires, and a continued exposure to the European heritage that comes alive for the essayist under the guise of ever so many names of authors and books. Toward the end of the autobiographical section young Eduardo has reached the awareness that was to remain one of the essential constants throughout his long literary career, namely the immersion in *his* city, "enormous city, without beauty, desertlike, valley of grey stone . . . filled with monotonous voices of ever so many newspapers, streets for furtive lovers, elegant cafés, hotels, and restaurants."[46] But the author's metaphysical anguish begins to rear its head as his metropolitan experience is channeled more and more into a complaisant bourgeois routine that decries the idealist in him. In closing this section he takes issue with his European self, and he decides that the tragic sense of life, the affinity for the original expression of his people, and the need to discover tangible evidence of this expression will carry him along the path leading to a twofold Argentina: the visible and the invisible land.

In the following chapters Mallea visualizes an Argentina filled with men and women who are very nearly replicas of those found in *The City on the Motionless River*. He ascribes to them a number of qualities, among which stand out such key characteristics as "dignity, aloofness, pride, even haughtiness," mixed with "a surprising amount of intelligence and an aptitude for assimilating culture."[47] One could easily speculate that most of these traits are the legacy of Mallea's paternal image and that in spite of an occasional allusion to the worker in the factory or on the farm the author has little knowledge to justify inclusion and portrayal of this type of Argentine in his national inventory. Reluctant to leave the city—a sterile yet compelling mistress—and prone to associate with people who act and talk on his level, his image of the visible Argentina is made up of an elite segment. What he finds in his sampling is a European order in an advanced state of crisis and dissolution, transplanted to a New World; he also sees evidence of crass materialism, a leftover from the *Conquistador* mentality. The sum total for Mallea amounts to a worn-out European mode that had been imposed on the New-World societies where it was being continued by the bourgeois element. What annoyed Mallea most, however, was the cloak of respectability wrapped around the dominant bourgeois *Weltanschauung*, a respectability concocted with "an encyclopedic and erudite appearance bereft of beliefs," an "artificial spirituality" promoted by "false Emersonians and perennial pragmatists," and, all in all, a false humanity.[48]

In a clear attempt at polarization, Mallea hopes to stem this tide of European materialism and false or worn-out humanism by producing the *true* visible Argentina and its spiritual powers. Thus he refers to "the authentic tradition, the land . . . the true roots in *our* songs, *our* dances, *our* cultural activities," all contaminated by the European malaise.[49] Writing now with heightened intensity Mallea raises a prophetic voice and repeatedly decries this contamination demanding a purification that would safeguard the "contaminated national sources of culture," revitalize the national language and pave the way for "true freedom of expression," an expression that would lead above all to an "austere and serene frame of mind."[50]

Mallea's authentic and visible Argentina stems naturally to a large extent from the invisible one. While true spiritual strength can be found in latent stages in the Argentine metropolis or such cities as Rosario, Córdoba, or Santa Fe, its roots would have to be deeply anchored in the earth or what Mallea later defines as "the ethical land," a sort of "moral hinterland holding untold riches in the untapped profundity of its womb."[51]

Not unexpectedly, Mallea now dons his traveling boots in order to cover the neglected hinterland and establish a meaningful contact with those who inherited the earth. Mallea the traveler reacts in a somewhat populist fashion to the surface symbols of his invisible Argentina. He quotes Walt Whitman's line "Me imperturb, standing at ease in nature" and witnesses the physical wonders of nature with the curious eyes of the newcomer: green pastures, moving cattle, fields of yellow grain, the rain, the sunset, a desert glow, and abrupt nightfall. In his lyric mood Mallea senses that the earth is becoming an alive and creative force that can easily be regarded as being the generator of *argentinidad:* "Instead of being docile, the land becomes active, it rises, takes shape, it is no longer just a ground for the galloping colt . . . it sheds its passive role and pursues the animal as well as the man . . . it looms so tall that the moon itself seems to be touched by its furrows."[52] Mallea's lyric progression includes those closely connected to this spiritually pregnant

land: "A man who tests this land, works it, nourishes it . . . almost
submerged in the secrecy of his task . . . filled with substantial humanity . . . whose very hands are roots . . . in a state of spiritual
affirmation embodying Ganivet's ethical element. . . ."[53]

Angel Ganivet's brand of history and historicity appealed to a
number of writers in the Hispanic world. The Spanish essayist's
search for a rational essence as a source for cultural power intrigued
those who were looking for their own people's identity. No doubt
what interested Mallea was Ganivet's insistence on a strong con-
centration of spiritual characteristics that would allow a nation to
survive as a cultural and even political unit. By concentrating on
these characteristics Mallea could make the difficult transition from
the spiritual land as a source for inspiration to the need for a national
cultural model while at the same time bypassing the hurdle of political patriotism. Thus he can go on to affirm that in his search for the
genuine *homo argentinus* he is not necessarily considering the peas-
ant, the landowner, or even the gaucho as a preferred category but
is rather looking for human beings who are blessed with a special
condition that will make them react positively to "the proper ambiance, form, and nature of the Argentine land," and conclude by
expressing the hope that from such beings "the path of history and
nationality will be charted."[54]

In this chapter as well as the following ones Mallea makes a
sustained effort to look at European heritage and thought as being
insufficient in order to satisfy the needs of a spiritualized Argentina.
In his declaration of faith he naturally cannot employ the discipline
of intellectual inquiry or the rigors of logic. In this he comes to join
the ranks of a group of Argentine writers that includes such divergent figures as Manuel Gálvez and Ezequiel Martínez Estrada, all
of whom prospered by seeking anti-intellectual solutions for Argentina and America. When Mallea states that the foreign intellectuals
who came to visit Argentina and examine its organic structure left
without having seen or understood the genuine Argentina,[55] he
lends his voice to the chorus of such nationalistic writers as Raúl
Scalabrini Ortiz and Pedro Orgambide who have proudly proc-
laimed the supremacy of native intuition over European knowledge.[56]

In the next chapters Mallea singles out two foreign men of letters,
the Baltic Count Herrman Keyserling and the American Waldo
Frank, who had written about the New World image and destiny

before visiting Mallea's homeland. The Argentine writer severely criticized Keyserling's *South American Meditations (Südameri-kanische Meditationen)* and chided the Baltic aristocrat for his morbid attraction toward an exuberant New World nature that lay in a state of chaotic decomposition. Since Mallea had already turned his back to the disintegrating order of a rapidly disintegrating Europe, he would obviously have to deride the count for his psychological analysis that ignored a preoccupation with both ethics and order. As was to be expected, Mallea favored Frank's theory of aesthetic evolution as displayed in *South American Journal.* Waldo Frank's view of the Americas as a new continent that should not imitate the respective Anglo-Saxon or Hispanic-Mediterranean cultures fit Mallea's theory of an autochthonous destiny for the New World, although neither the American nor the Argentine writer went on to explain how the synthesis of their legacies would be accomplished.

In the final chapters of *History of an Argentine Passion* the author gravitates again toward a personal search for manifestations of the genuine Argentina when making his *Winterreise* to the hinterland. He visits small, sleepy towns with their deserted streets and colonial churches; he talks to the young man in a Spanish-type inn; and he sees a number of small farms sprinkled with fruit trees and vegetable gardens. But wherever he goes, our traveler encounters an opaque indifference, an absence of stability, and a state of constant slumber. The human representatives prove equally devoid of a state of fervor envisioned by our urban visitor. One such rustic figure is compared to the land itself by Mallea as he and a group of travelers try to have him share the secrets of the land with them: ". . . each word seemed to battle an overwhelming interior obstacle. His earthlike lips hardly moved. There were long intervals between each word seemed to battle an overwhelming interior obstacle. His earthlike lips hardly moved. There were long intervals between each word. In spite of my insistence it was impossible to extricate a meaning from this inert mass of human flesh. We left conscious of our total failure."[57]

Argentina was the realization that a rustic mode of existence per se would neither produce a desirable state of nobility nor a spirit of abnegation and self-sacrifice. However, for Mallea the rustic condition still remained a logical basis for a process of purification and spiritual germination far from the madding crowd for the city dweller in search of *argentinidad.*

Toward the end of *History of an Argentine Passion* the author sums up his position vis-à-vis his recent European experience by seeking refuge in an inner reality devoid of European tradition or knowledge. Stylistically we find a repetition and intensification of key words or phrases: "I lived in relative poverty, unpretentiously, almost always taciturn and unyielding . . . I rarely talked to people, in fact, I wanted to suppress the spoken word . . . or substitute it with a sign corresponding to something deep in my imagination."[58]

Behind this confessional tone lies, of course, an inner agony, as Professor Polt put it.[59] After crossing the Atlantic he found himself "empty-handed"; that is to say, without his European intellectual baggage. This emptiness coupled with the blatantly meaningless routine of his bourgeois *porteño* world produced the inner agony that became transubstantiated into an outcry of metaphysical hunger. The words roll off with accustomed vehemence: ". . . ardor, contempt, fury, hope, despair, self-criticism, insomnia, pondering, stubbornness, cruel delight, the hunger to touch the earth, touch humanity . . . fear, courage, hesitation, hunger, always hunger. . . ."[60]

The final pages of the book find him completing the cycle, back on his city streets, walking aimlessly into the night while looking for "my people, my external homeland, my sensitive nation. . . ."[61] Mallea's contemporary, the Argentine essayist and critic Bernardo Canal Feijoo, wrote that *History of an Argentine Passion* combined the symbolic identification of a personal quest with a national one thus creating a truly historical awareness.[62] In spite of Mallea's hunger for spiritualization it could hardly be decided that his search for the as yet invisible Argentina leads him on the trail to unearthing the Argentine *Volksgeist*, an attitude closely linked to that of the European romantics in the nineteenth century. That this search should prove to be inconclusive finds corroboration in the reappearance of this theme in later works.

CHAPTER 3

The Cosmopolitan Spirit

I Fiesta in November

AFTER the appearance of *History of an Argentine Passion* Mallea found himself emerging as a major force on the Argentine intellectual and literary scene. In the brief period of three years he had published a novel, an outstanding collection of short stories, and a book of essays that was to become a landmark in the emergence of national awareness as well as historicity. At the same time, his position as editor of the "Literary Supplement" of *La Nación,* his close friendship and collaboration with Victoria Ocampo, owner-director of *Sur,* the highly influential journal and publishing house, and his intimate ties to the literary establishment had given him prestige, power, and a certain degree of influence. Both *European Nocturne* and *The City on the Motionless River* had been initially printed by Editorial Sur. Sudamericana, Argentina's foremost publishing house over the last forty-some years immediately brought out its own edition of *The City on the Motionless River.* Espasa Calpe, Spain's largest book publisher with a branch in Buenos Aires began to issue its edition of *History of an Argentine Passion* with a prologue by Francisco Romero, Argentina's leading philosopher and a disciple of the Spanish thinker Ortega y Gasset. The Argentine Espasa Calpe also reprinted *Stories of a Desperate Englishwoman,* now with a new prologue by the author.

At the age of thirty-four Mallea had achieved an enviable record; yet his inner self was hardly satisfied. He had gained literary laurels without allowing the smallest concession to the prevailing artistic fashions or stylistic dicta. He had written without ulterior motives or considerations, true to his ever increasing existential agony that forced him to follow his self-imposed quests at times elusive and beyond his grasp. Yet in his daily experience he felt condemned to endure the constant encounter and friction with the bourgeois world

56

to which he inextricably belonged; and this unsatisfactory state prompted him time and again to attempt a transcendence of this unsatisfactory situation in order to reach spiritual immanence. The obstacles placed on his road to the metaphysical bridge leading to the promised shores of the true Argentina and its genuine people loomed as large as ever. However, this impasse resulted in Mallea's eagerness to continue his quest and to give it added form and substance. Thus at the age of thirty-five Mallea sought a way to produce a restatement and an intensification of earlier themes, symbols, and metaphors. Within a relatively short period of time he was able to bring out a new novel, *Fiesta in November (Fiesta en noviembre)*, as well as a slender volume of essays, *Meditation at the Sea Shore (Meditación en la costa)*.

Amado Alonso, the famous Spanish literary critic who spent many years teaching in Argentine universities, leaving his imprint on a whole generation of new writers like Ernesto Sábato and Enrique Anderson Imbert, said of *Fiesta in November* that it represents a fictionalization of *History of an Argentine Passion* and is essentially a dramatized confrontation of the visible and the invisible land.[1] Many elements in the novel impress the reader as being typically Mallean: the hermetic protagonists, the shallow or insensitive secondary characters, the bourgeois setting, and the grave language. Wealthy Mrs. de Rague gives a party at which the cream of *porteño* society was to be present: ambassadors, judges, financiers, politicians, artists, and landed gentry, all in all "a bathed and lotioned bunch" exchanging inane remarks and making pseudoartistic comments on the *objects d'art* that so profusely adorn the downstairs and upstairs of the de Rague mansion. Mrs. de Rague as well as her less obtrusive husband behave like classic oligarchs displaying their affluence by exhibiting an overwhelming assortment of art treasures from a huge canvas by Titian to a giant Louis Quatorze chandelier. Neither they nor their illustrious guests pay any attention to the intrinsic value of these objects: for them it is sufficient that art exudes an expensive and exclusive air. When Lintas, the male protagonist, dares to point out the artificially inflated value of one of the paintings the hostess becomes deeply offended because her prestige, residing entirely in the monetary value of her acquisitions, has been placed in jeopardy. Lintas feels that he must leave; and the hostess' daughter, Marta de Rague, takes it upon herself to accompany the reluctant art critic. Both Lintas and his female companion are typical Mallean characters: reserved, introspect, well educated, sensitive, and intelligent. Yet both are incomplete beings in that they constitute islands: "Neither he nor she were going to yield to the other. Both were by nature reserved, asocial. He had made the first gesture by getting close to her and hated himself for abdicating his cavalier solitude . . . two beings defeated by their mutual mistrust."[2]

But, as the evening progresses and Marta de Rague decides to accompany Lintas to his artist's studio, their dialogue begins to unlock aspects of their lives that are keeping both of them prisoners of the past. Lintas, not unlike the author, made a trip to Europe in 1934 in pursuit of the origins of Western artistic thought and found instead a state of grave disorder and an absolute lack of harmony. He happened to fall in love with a somewhat exotic woman from an Eastern European country; but her intellectual propensities and domineering nature soon produced boredom and fatigue in him. Returning to his native country he sought refuge in his art; and what might have been previously a strong vocation now became a feverish activity possibly to deceive the growing restlessness within. "My work became a very efficient opiate," he confesses to Marta de Rague.[3]

After a long interval of silence both begin to formulate a tenuous basis for their future action. But when Lintas talks about overcoming his inner barriers in order to eliminate what he calls "his aloof consciousness," Marta voices a warning:

Be careful that your lovely vision of human communion does not begin by dividing you within yourself. You gave me a picture of a man who wants to transcend his condition at all costs. . . . Be careful. Our life is not unlike a bag, and there is no merit in offering it to someone else if it should be empty. . . . To be true to one's self, then, is also taken to reflect one's good qualities. So why not concentrate on this essence instead of looking for it outside of one's self?[4]

When Lintas in a very pensive mood objects that "one cannot speed up one's process of maturation," she agrees in principle but cautions him once more: "One has to watch this maturing process. A lack of action might bring about the disease of the mind, but action born out of blind ambition can sicken it even more. Be careful that instead of action per se you are not nourishing hatred."[5]

Marta de Rague's advice represents the possibility of moving toward a form of self-fulfillment that was not available to Adrian, the protagonist of *European Nocturne*. But in order to reach this desired state one must intensify one's intrinsic qualities rather than remain searching for a romantic quintessence. Probably the most incisive line of the whole novel consists of Marta telling Lintas that "the trouble is nobody wants to be himself. You for instance."[6] Mallea here opens his eyes to a problem that is rooted in a deep dissatisfaction with himself, a problem that has led him to ignore the social self in favor of a metaphysical self that would hopefully emerge by virtue of an almost mystical transformation triggered by a process of self-sacrifice and final purification. As a typical Mallean protagonist, Lintas is fascinated by the possibility of "becoming," an attitude that perforce excludes the exploration and acceptance of the true self. As the novel progresses the distance between the true and the projected self increases, Lintas' self-searching process intensifies, and Marta de Rague's advice falls on deaf ears.

As to the structure of the novel, Mallea invented a contrapuntal device to dramatize thematic development. Two contrasts are established: one concerning characterization, the other one plot.

Marta de Rague has a sister, named Brenda, who just underwent one more abortion and is recovering in the bedroom of some midwife. Marta tries to comfort her and promises to keep her new affair a secret. But she also feels like an impotent onlooker who has witnessed another failure, an alteration of the natural order due to social codes and existing stigma. Her feelings of impotence contain an admixture of quiet, because over the years she has not been able to provide the smallest measure of guidance or influence concerning the human being that has been sharing the family's home and living in the room next to hers. For Marta the mutilation of the organic growth in her sister's womb is accompanied by the mutilation of the mind; and Brenda's condition furnishes Marta with the irrefutable proof that each of them is formed to the point of having become a finished product, unalterable and condemned to be herself in spite of defects or shortcomings.

On the narrative level two seemingly unrelated episodes emerge, neither of them forming part of the main plot yet both overshadowing the basically static confrontation of the protagonists Lintas and Marta de Rague. The first of these episodes takes place in a remote European country torn by internal strife. In a given town a group of

soldiers invades the modest home of a nameless man. It is his turn to
be taken to a deserted place outside of the town and be executed.
The man had been in the midst of adding a line to his unfinished
poem and was holding a piece of bread in the other hand. On the
way to his execution the man projects his sensations of the act of
dying and conjures up the final scene in which his purple blood will
cover the white shirt and motionless body, much like the child and
the man whose bodies he just saw on his way out of town. In his final
moment the man's fist clutches the piece of bread while imagination, horror, reality, and death converge, becoming one. Mallea has
fragmented the whole episode throughout the novel in order to
produce a recurring contrast with the elegant milieu at the de
Rague's reception. The episode's stark action and somber mood
serve as a notable counterpoint to the meaningless goings-on at the
party. It is also quite obvious that the unfinished poetry as well as
the piece of bread serve to symbolize mankind's basic needs: the
nourishment of body and soul.[7]

The second episode is told to Marta de Rague by Lintas himself. A
short time ago a European immigrant who owned a bookstore near
Lintas' residence was attacked by a pseudofascist mob that was bent
on "cleaning" Argentina of pernicious foreign influences. The owner
was kidnapped, severely beaten, and a considerable number of his
books destroyed. Two months later he died, not so much due to the
physical beating as to a broken spirit. Ever since that time his widow
has broken out in nightly shrieks that reach Lintas' bedroom, echo-
ing the fear and terror of a crushed humanity.

On the note of suffering, despair, and death both episodes converge onto the central axis of the novel. Both indicate a general state
of inhumanity in the Western world that in 1938 was rapidly waxing
into the holocaust that became known as World War II and that had
its bloody preamble during the Spanish Civil War from 1936 to
1937. Whereas many Latin American intellectuals became directly
or indirectly involved with political events and most of them took a
stand on the fratricidal struggle in Spain, it was not in Mallea's
make-up to do so. As an example, the Chileans Gabriela Mistral and
Pablo Neruda and the Guatemalan Miguel Angel Asturias—all three
Nobel Prize winners—worked actively for the republican government of Spain, and notable Argentine writers tried their best to help
their Spanish colleagues to settle in Buenos Aires when the republican cause was lost. However, Mallea's expressed views on the dan-

gers of demagogic populism and dictatorial mass politics put him clearly on record against the diverse types of fascism that were spreading across the map of Europe in the late 1930s. It seems fairly obvious that the nameless man who was executed with an unfinished poem and a piece of bread in his hands was Federico García Lorca, Spain's most treasured modern poet, who had attacked the false values of traditional Spanish society in such plays as *The House of Bernarda Alba* and who died before a firing squad in 1936 when the specter of civil war had just begun to spread chaos and destruction throughout parts of the Spanish land.

Once more, Mallea has established the disintegration of Europe's old order and juxtaposed this condition with an Argentine sequence. The poet who died riddled with rifle bullets and the bookstore owner lying on the grass of a *porteño* park have both shed the same precious blood and had their life extinguished by the same forces of evil: "The world was filled with shouts, shapes, voices, silence, crime, struggle, madness, fury. . . ."[8] Yet the elegant, chattering, prim, and proper ladies and gentlemen who milled around de Rague's *fiesta* were not aware of these signals. To recognize these signals and to react to them with the right awareness, then, would be the task of the genuine Argentines.

II Meditation at the Sea Shore

Definitely launched on a full-fledged writing career Mallea felt the need to restate and reinterpret themes he had partially developed in earlier essays. Thus *Meditation at the Sea Shore (Meditación en la costa)* was begun in early 1938, before he turned once more to fiction, this time to reach the peak of his first novelistic cycle with *The Bay of Silence*.

Francisco Ayala, the well-known Spanish novelist and critic, who came to know Mallea rather well over the years, saw in *Meditation at the Sea Shore* a renewed effort to evolve an Argentine mode of being out of a badly deteriorated European heritage. Ayala regards Mallea's European explorations as a necessary initiation rite that would prepare the ground for a national sequel.[9] Mallea indeed meditates on life along the Atlantic coast while, with an eye cocked at the distant shores of Europe, he ponders the confluence of New and Old Worlds. But after the visions of ancient town squares in Belgium or Gothic cathedrals in France are conjured up and fade away, and after the organic disorder of Europe is diagnosed once

more, the author focuses on the process involved in the making of an
argentinidad that reflects his concern with a noble and spiritual state
of mind on the individual as well as on the collective plane.

Looking at the Europeans and sons of Europeans who disem-
barked in the New World on the docks of Buenos Aires Mallea
wonders what their motives for coming were and how they could
have escaped the malaise of disintegration and disorder that was
infecting the Old World. Mallea took a very negative view of the
wholesale importation of materialistic-oriented masses that would
flood and contaminate the "Garden of Eden," thus spoiling its
spiritual potential. Here Mallea appears as the forerunner of Martínez Estrada and H. A. Murena who in the 1950s and 1960s
reaffirmed the Edenic theme as a blueprint for America's road to
regeneration while rejecting what Martínez Estrada called "the rape
of the land." But Mallea was even more alarmed by the prospect of
Argentina's admitting human beings manipulated by social and
political systems of the totalitarian and populist variety that had
begun to proliferate in the Europe of the 1930s. Instead of dealing
with collectively formed entities Mallea would rather begin by taking the individual and build a *Gemeinschaft*, a true community,
based on the diverse individual qualities whose sum total would
exceed the isolated quantity. Although he fails to furnish the reader
with a workable program leading to this *Gemeinschaft*, he does at
least assert that "every person represents a unique world, as
uniquely as every fingerprint, and one cannot then imagine a collective reality unless it be in the form of a well balanced concert that
renders possible the respective essence and existence of everyone."[10] The concept of populist power, then, loomed as a dangerous
manifestation to Mallea; and it mattered little whether this power
was achieved by political coercion handed down from a dictatorial
government or simply occurred due to sheer mass pressure resulting from social or economic demands.

Appropriately enough we find repeated references to Ortega y
Gasset's *The Revolt of the Masses* in which the Spanish philosopher
expressed his preoccupation with the new era of majorities' rights
and the infringement of the individual's freedom of action. From
Mallea's point of view, as he sat at the shore overlooking the open
sea and scanning the distant horizon of his native land, the demo-
graphic compactness found in Western Europe seemed like a per-

ennial tyranny over the senses as well as sensitivity and reinforced his aversion to the apparent need for accommodation and compromise resulting from the interaction of human beings who are constantly forced upon one another. In other words, human ecology and spatial scarcity had occluded the "magical" and regenerative powers of the land. For Mallea Argentina's spiritual order was in danger of being invaded by the sheer weight of the masses, masses that had become a new cultural force in that they were beginning to impose a tasteless and materialistic way of life on a hapless society, thus producing the feared "invasion of humanity" due to the waning of Ortega y Gasset's elite.[11] According to Mallea this unfortunately becomes compounded and aggravated by the ever-increasing output of mass media and its accumulative impact on the average individual. He talks about the contamination resulting from constant daily exposure to unavoidable forms of information, communication, or instruction, all releasing floods of meanings and symbols whose intrinsic values become blurred, diminished, or altogether lost. The final result of these processes would be a forceable decline or elimination of one's emotive capacity to react fully and significantly to the major stimulus inherent in word-symbols or humanistic thought. Mallea's summation of these processes forms a devastatingly negative trinity: "hatred, death, and tragic sterility."[12]

In the latter part of *Meditation at the Sea Shore* Mallea attempts to apply the insight gained in his European travels to remedy Argentina's incompleteness. Staring into the waves of the south Atlantic from the very edge of the pampas, he takes stock of the physical and social realities of his country and in doing so experiences a great need of finding ways to eliminate the foreign or negative elements that have been left behind by the bearers of "worn-out European civilizations."[13] Following the contours of the land from Cape Horn to the northern jungles touching Brazil and crossing the vast prairies up to the foothills of the Andean mountain range next to Chile, Mallea envisions an Argentine nation containing some fifty million people, homogeneous and cohesive, strongly inspired by its national destiny, and nourished by the spirit arising from the land, "the physical land, the ethical land, the personal land."[14] In Mallca's mind the interaction between the inhabitant and the land is vital. Unless this state is attained, he argues, the Argentine people will live in a most illusory stage of development, since there can be no national awareness without communing with the geographical foundations of the country.[15]

At this juncture it should be pointed out that Mallea's nationalism is of a peculiar brand. He does not take issue with a topic that seems obligatory for most nationalists in Latin America, namely the matter of economic exploitation by the so-called imperialistic powers, a theme close to the hearts of such Argentine contemporaries as Manuel Gálvez and Raúl Scalabrini Ortíz. In fact, Mallea states quite openly that it is not important whether the railroads or utilities are owned by foreign corporations or Argentine businessmen. What is needed foremost is the reconquest of the Argentine people's spirit, the territorial spirit.

Here Mallea touches upon a most vexing problem, one that has been scrutinized and explored in the days of Haman, Herder, and the German romantics around 1800: the redemptive power of nature. Nineteenth-century romanticism viewed nature as a great and ennobling force, a concept that people like Angel Ganivet in Spain and Maurice Barrès in France amplified around the turn of this century in order to demonstrate that the moral and spiritual strength stemming from the identification with the native soil would overcome the countless ills plaguing the modern technological societies, especially the malaise of uprootedness. Barríes furnished possibly the perfect example of tragedy ensuing from the severing of ties with the land and moving to a cosmopolitan center, in this case Paris. Although Barrès' *The Uprooted* has not been accepted by most critics as the model for Mallea's tragic vision of Buenos Aires, in both authors the city as a negative influence on the spirit of the land looms extremely large; and both men have refused to recognize that the city as a technological or industrial center is the key to modern ecology. After all, the big city as a provider of jobs, education, and artistic activities would have to be taken into consideration when realistically assessing the value and function of urban centers. In this respect, Mallea's condemnation of the city and his search for the "ethical land" seems but a neoromantic formula.

Mass society hardly lends itself to be swayed by the spirit of the land. It took a small and homogeneous group, a clan, to produce norms, beliefs, and behavior based on ecological adaptation that could be shared by all of the members. The shared characteristics, based on terrain, climate, vegetation, and territorial limitations influenced cultural expression and provided common denominators for the individual. The interaction with nature and the social group furnished indeed a *Volksgeist*, a communal spirit, that proved to be so dear to the romantic, always in search of genuine folkloric and literary expression and its national origin. In modern mass societies, however, the spirit of a nation is subject to an array of outside influences. Cultural stimuli in the shape of "foreign" books, magazines, records, films, and other mass-media instruments create a lasting impact in the form of adoption, adaptation, or transculturation. Thus the quest for an *argentinidad* nourished primarily by the spirit of the land becomes seriously hampered, especially in a cosmopolitan center like Buenos Aires with its open society and dynamic culture patterns. Yet Buenos Aires has sheltered the true Mallean personages who, like the author, are totally "civilized" beings, more familiar with the sidewalks, offices, cafés, and apartment dwellings than the fields or pastures of the hinterland. Since he hopes to mobilize their outward talents and inner resources to attain a state of grace, Mallea returns time and again to the city and its soulless melancholy. "Buenos Aires showed its desolation along the enormous extension of the city converging onto the arid plaza, where the tower erected by the British constitutes a final melancholic sign from which one can see the ships in the harbor ready to depart for unknown lands."[16]

In *Meditation at the Sea Shore*, as in previous works such as *The City on the Motionless River*, the city appears contaminated by non-Argentine substances and filled with bourgeois materialism, both antitheses of the Argentine psyche that was established in *History of an Argentine Passion*. But a national psyche must be fed by myths and rituals whose nature is collective and communal, as Philip Wheelwright well observed in *The Burning Fountain*, in order to bind people and spur the collective imagination.[17] Mallea strongly favors the formation of a national psyche or character, but he is very carefully avoiding any political or populist manipulation that might achieve a level of patriotism on which his *argentinidad* could conceivably flourish. While he specifically refers to the greatness of such national leaders as General San Martín, Father Mamerto Esquiù, or President Domingo Faustino Sarmiento, he clearly avoids the utilization of a sociopolitical structure to arrive at the true nature of his *argentinidad*.[18] Rejecting a nationalistic solution through populist means Mallea can only fall back onto his old formula: the ethical land appealing to the sensitive intellect of the urban Argentine.

III   The Bay of Silence

Mallea's next work, *The Bay of Silence*, appeared in October, 1940. Although the substance of this novel shows a greater complexity and a more detailed effort to portray a vast setting in time and space than his previous fiction, a number of critics have voiced the opinion that the work is too lengthy and too amorphous. A paraphrase of Patrick Dudgeon's account of the novel might be of value. The book contains some five hundred and eighty pages in the edition brought out by Sudamericana. Divided into three parts, "The Young Men" ("Los Jóvenes"), "The Islands" ("Las Islas"), and "The Defeated" ("Los Derrotados"), *The Bay of Silence* covers some thirteen years, from 1926 to 1939, and takes place in Argentina as well as Northern Europe. The novel has the structural shape of a diary, the diary of one Martín Tregua, a former law student living in Buenos Aires, who is trying to make a name for himself as a novelist. Tregua resembles to a large degree the author in that he reveals his doubts and goals, even his anguish, in a fashion established in earlier works of Mallea. Tregua, coeditor of a new magazine called *Basta*, lives surrounded by intellectual companions and finds himself in the process of writing a long novel entitled "The 40 Nights of Juan Argentino." This novel aims to portray the national archetype based on the humble, ordinary, and silent Argentine who stands juxtaposed by the bureaucratic, corrupt, and internationally oriented governing oligarchy.[19] Dudgeon goes on to say that *The Bay of Silence* reads as if written as an intellectual exercise carried out in somewhat of a void, written for the author's sake, perhaps for the purpose of getting "what had been long worrying him off his chest, without weighing the likes and dislikes of the public . . . [since] the philosophical passages are beyond the ordinary reader who would in any case hardly sympathize with Martín Tregua and his grievances."[20] Tregua's efforts to overcome a national state of inertia, indifference, or even corruption give an appearance of futility: he as well as his creator express their naiveté when they assume that it takes but an avant-garde magazine propelled by a handful of unknown young intellectuals to bring about radical changes in the traditional power structure as well as ingrained social attitudes. Mallea, of course, is not a revolutionary pamphleteer in the style of Charles Dickens or the Argentine Roberto Payró, as Patrick Dudgeon observes. Rather, he writes from the position of the preexistential intellectual who is compelled to express his fatigue, revulsion, and *ennui* as he explores the *condition humaine* of his society, a society that embodies the deepening malaise of the modern Western World.

Dudgeon made a general assessment of the positive impact of the novel by calling it the "biography of a soul" that shows a remarkable similarity to the better works of Henry James when it comes to the long and minute dissections of the protagonist's mind as well as a constant preoccupation with the experience of the artist.[21] Mallea has indeed sacrificed action and plot development as he gained in texture and depth characterization by perceiving and portraying the world that encompasses the writer-protagonist and his creations. He works here with a deep attention to detail, taking great pains to recreate the topography of Buenos Aires in the first and third division of the novel. Martín Tregua and some of his young intellectual‹ companions live in Doña Ava's boardinghouse in the actual port district of the immense city, filled with sailors' bars, immigrant cafés, and cheap hotels. Tregua, like Mallea himself, proves to be the eternal wanderer who day or night covers the Barrio Norte, Florida, or Corrientes Streets. The comings and goings of Tregua and his friends stand out against a live background. We are shown a wide variation of urban types and their social settings: exhausted and famished night watchmen waiting for a streetcar; a mailman narrowly escaping being run over by a swerving car; sailors making the rounds of the "joints" near Tregua's house; a high official stepping into his old and noisy Austin; elegantly dressed members ascending the steps to the exclusive Club de Armas on Corrientes Street;[22] a new dawn finding the night owls and men about town leaving the night clubs, jaded and tired. Mallea follows his characters setting up their surroundings. The tavern on Lavalle Street where Tregua and others plot the course of their magazine *Basta* is described with meticulous care; the same applies to the food they consume. One of Mallea's habits throughout his entire literary career has been the propensity of placing his characters within the framework of a café or restaurant and dwelling on the consumption of food and drink as if this activity held a ritualistic meaning for civilized beings.

But the novel is foremost a confession, the confession of an "en-
fant du siècle," a century in which the lines between fiction and
reality are often blurred; and here Mallea shows himself to be modern in that he endows his protagonist with an autonomous power, a
technique that has been foreshadowed by an Unamuno or Pirandello. An example of this autonomy has been aptly cited by Dudgeon who looks at Tregua's stay at his friend Ferrier's house in
Brussels in "The Islands," the second part of the novel. In roaming
through the bookshelves in Ferrier's library Tregua discovers James
Joyce's *Ulysses*, whereupon he reacts to Joyce's prose with a personal totality:

Tregua is lingering over Joyce, and Mallea is suggesting that the criticism of
Joyce's work is the thoughts going on in Tregua's head, which shows the
importance both creator and created attach to this writer. It is true that
Tregua could hardly have thought so much, and that in so orderly a fashion . . . but it should be noticed that a moment of time comes to an end
with the conclusion of the opinion on Joyce, that is to say, Tregua does not
think for a moment and then Ferrier comes back and the conversation
between them continues. The opinion on Joyce is really meant to be Tregua's thoughts at that moment, and the space allotted to it is a confession
that Tregua is particularly interested in this European writer and may want
to adopt some of his experiment to his own purposes. A novel of this kind, a
novel about a novelist, must contain such passages. They make *La bahía de
silencio* of the greatest interest to the literary reader however much they
may cut it off from readers who demand the adventures and excitement of
the Robinson Crusoe type.[23]

A somewhat different focus on this novel is furnished by one of
the deans of Argentine letters, the essayist and critic Bernardo
Canal Feijóo. Before taking up cardinal aspects pertaining to structure and characterization in *The Bay of Silence*, Canal Feijóo
examines the situation of the novel in the Western World and finds
that there is a continuously growing gap between the expectancy of
the traditional reader and the course plotted by authors who write to
satisfy their inner anguish, bypassing a rational novelistic development and concentrating on a fractional, inner reality.[24] For Canal
Feijóo, Mallea's work exudes a veritable furor that takes the unsus-
pecting reader by surprise. It is the furor of the author's own holy
war with himself coupled with the license—an arrogant one—to
suspend action in order to make endless pronouncements on art,

letters, or history. Since Mallea's holy war is fought on the bat-
tlefield of the novel itself, the latter is bound to suffer.[25] Here Canal
Feijóo's view coincides with that of critics like Professor Polt who
hold that it is Mallea's tendency to novelize his essays and as a
consequence to produce a hybrid form that escapes the tenets of a
novel in the traditional sense. As Polt states, "[Mallea] has not only
repeated his themes but has also insisted on presenting in many of
his novels (notably *La bahía de silencio*) ideological questions unrelated to the lives of his spokesmen. . . . This all-absorbing subjec-
tivity is the greatest danger to the author's fiction; for, although the
novel is a flexible genre, it *is* fiction, not essay or autobiography.
Mallea's novels tend to cross that boundary. . . .[26]

The problems of Mallea's novelistic structure show a corresponding counterpart on the level of character development. Tregua and
his circle of "Los Jóvenes" enact an Argentine awareness that in-
hibits their personal development. Canal Feijóo attempts a blanket
critique on this subject:

None of the characters seems to have a known profession or occupation—
they live perhaps on private income—they are found in cafés, restaurants,
or somewhere in Europe, where they talk about the problems of their
country, agreeing always that something ought to be done, although they
never can find out exactly what that is. Basically they are extremely seden-
tary and verbose; they cannot resist the temptation of a good meal and hold
forth admirably and in the most lucid fashion about grave matters, so that
they might well be considered Platonists. This seems to be their sole *raison
d'être*. They call themselves true Argentines and feel this condition with
great pride; however, their daily lives are surrounded by foreign elements.
No doubt they are right in that it is one thing to love one's fatherland and
quite another to drink bad domestic champagne, smoke smelly local cigars,
or wear terrible homespun clothes. . . . Obviously they cannot take responsibility for the lack of a strongly developed national industry. . . . They
never quite come to terms with life's realities; rather, they have an overwhelming need to clothe reality in erudite terms, in lecture form, and
generally in a foreign language. They distinctly comprehend only what
reaches them in a written or painted medium; the immediate world remains
untouched and ignored. . . . They are full of informative experiences, un-
forgettable remembrances of what is absent, of happy memories; all this
material fills their souls to such an extent that there remains no room for the
other: the authentic life. Their final misfortune consists of not being able to
forget what they have accumulated inside, everything that was borrowed or
foreign to them and to their authentic selves. They are characters who know

all voices but their own; and thus they naturally fall into their own abysmal silence . . . they talk beautifully and brilliantly, they love stupidly, they end up pathetically. They are never at a loss for words but afterward they just disappear; they are like human fireflies, they need the night to make their appearance known; the bright daylight erases them; they are left with their memories and have this moment; what they lack is their own future.[27]

The Argentine critic's comments seem caustic and perhaps a trifle harsh. Yet, he focuses on a novelistic weakness that struck other critics similarly. John Polt writes that ". . . [Mallea's] willingness to express himself in his novels is almost unlimited, his capacity for empathy, for inventing a character who is not himself, and projecting himself into that character, is modest, in spite of fragmentary successes. . . ."[28] The Argentine intellectuals of "Los Jóvenes" and their European counterparts in "Las Islas" share the conditions enumerated by Canal Feijóo and Polt. Mallea appears to need these characters in order to portray what Professor Fernando Alegría calls Mallea's "testimonial of conscience."[29] Alegría goes on to explain the relationship between the characters and the Mallean conscience:

Men and women come flowing out of his pen to measure the validity of his arguments in strictly intellectual duels. On a modern stage they would all wear the same tragic mask. Their worlds might differ but the spirit is identical. Heroes and villains, victors and victims, visionaries, those who are indifferent, sentimental, or stoic, none of them manages to become fully individualized; in fact, they only achieve an attitude that constitutes a reflection of the tormented narrator. . . . In the midst of his creation Mallea stands alone, surrounded by echoes and gestures that are but a substitute for his desperation.[30]

Aloof and wrapped up within his speculations, Tregua appears indeed as the author's projected self; moreover, the reader experiences the thoughts and actions of the other characters through Tregua, and they, in turn, only live as projections of the main character, most notably in the case of the female. Fernando Alegría observed very accurately that Mallea's female protagonists, Marta de Rague in *Fiesta in November* and Gloria Bambil in the *Bay of Silence*, represent a highly stylized image that actually becomes a stereotype. He could have easily included Miss Ira Dardington in *European Noc-*

turne and most of the women in *The City on the Motionless River*, from Cristiana Ruiz to Ana Borel. Alegría gives us her composite picture:

We soon learn to recognize this image: it is that of a woman of noble stature, with long and slender legs, an athletic mien but always somewhat wistful, who walks with her hands lost in the pockets of her sports jacket . . . it is always the same one. She is more intelligent than her male counterpart, more mature in expressing her emotions, more deeply conscious of the buried secrets of the invisible Argentina, moving from one café to another, from city to city, enveloped in a cloud of smoke from European cigarettes, laden with symbols like antique jewelry, and listening to the dissatisfaction of the hero who in Mallea's novels never ceases to be a sort of adolescent.[31]

In asking a final question, namely, of what does Mallea's invisible Argentina really consist, how can he reach this elusive spiritual center, and for what purpose, Alegría joins the queries of such critics as Canal Feijóo and Polt. Yet, beyond the essaylike tone, the dialectic discourse, and the repeating characters lie themes, images, and figures that allow for adroit explanations. A number of important observations can be made concerning temporal and spatial placement, narration, typology, and a view of various characters as symbols, as performed by Professor Herbert Gillessen in a fairly recent study.[32]

As to chronology, the novel encompasses over thirteen years, from 1926 to 1939 or the eve of World War II. While the first part, "Los Jóvenes," comprises about eight years, the second book, "Las Islas," accounts but for a few months, and then the last division, "Los Derrotados," lasts roughly five years. Thus the time element clearly favors Mallea's native soil, and the European experience looms largely like an interlude, an intermittent episode that gives added meaning to the Argentine segments. As in *Meditation on the Sea Shore*, the writer's European confrontation helped him to get a clearer perspective concerning the cultural state of his homeland. Mallea himself states that *The Bay of Silence*

registers many of the things I saw in Belgium and Italy, or, better said, many of the things about which I meditated while there; and a good deal of all this had to do with the European world that I saw during the months of my stay in 1934. I wrote *The Bay of Silence* in Buenos Aires starting with the second book, "Las Islas." I felt depressed and tired . . . until I inter-

rupted my work to recover in a sea resort in the southern part of the Buenos
Aires province, called Monte Hermoso. There I spent my days in melancholy and sadness, a state of mind that would be later reflected in the third
part of the novel.[33]

Apparently Mallea's inner reality during this period was instrumental in his fashioning a dual pessimistic condition: a European and an
Argentine one, both straining under grave and unsolvable crises.

Geographic space, according to Professor Gillessen, becomes
transfigured in the novel. Just as happened with time, space becomes relative, actually neutralized by inner unrest. Awareness and
the outer world are fused, but the outer world is determined by the
dictates of the inner placelessness. Only the meeting places count.
But encounter for Mallea means always an encounter with himself
because there is no transition into someone else, only a shared chaos
and silence.[34] The local scene in the first and third divisions has
been outlined earlier in this chapter; it amounts to Mallea's selected
portions of his eternal Buenos Aires, the obligatory background for
Tregua and his young friends. The European theater includes a
short stay in Paris and Como after which the protagonist travels to
Brussels where he finds a milieu and setting akin to that of his native
city, that is to say, a physical and social environment that allows for a
life-style in which monologues as well as dialogues on Mallea's favorite subjects ranging from literature to morality or politics can pre-
dominate.

The narrative framework contains two unusual features, namely
the use of a confessional context and the insertion of a novel within
the novel. Actually written in the form of the first person singular,
the author addresses the mysterious and idealized *usted*, the woman
whom Tregua meets at the beginning of the long novel in a flower
shop in downtown Buenos Aires. The reader who has built an inventory of Mallea's leading female characters will find in this new and
elusive figure an intensification of previously apparent attributes;
aloof, filled with an inner remoteness, aristocratic to the point of
arrogance, married into one of Argentina's oldest families, she reappears at intervals throughout the work. Her noble traits seem to
qualify her perfectly for the role of symbolizing the essence of a
national spirit as postulated in *History of an Argentine Passion*.
Professor Gillessen who has dwelled at length on the female characterization in *The Bay of Silence* sees in the *usted* a prototype that

lends itself to be the perfect recipient of all the usual and aesthetic manifestations that are dear to Mallea.[35] Lovely and proud, filled with a cold beauty and apparently untouched by the baser passions of mankind, she seems to be in many ways the female counterpart of the author himself. Could it be that Mallea has invented the *usted* as an extension, a projection of himself in order to confess with and to himself? Gillessen, who has explored the symbolization of the *usted* to the fullest,[36] shows how this figure takes on the characteristics of Carl Jung's anima and becomes a partner in Mallea's dialogue, "a new Beatrice, a new savior, the objectivized anima of the ego in search of itself."[37] The *usted* character, then, differs essentially from that of the second female protagonist in this novel, Gloria Bambil. Although she shares some of the author's favorite qualifications, is proud, silent, suffering, and proves to be also essentially tragic, she lacks two great qualities: the powers of love and redemption. Gloria Bambil is a solitary being, described as fashioned of cold sorrow and tedium, whose ever increasing sense of alienation drives her to committing suicide. While she also has been identified as the symbol of the invisible Argentina, her regeneration was never achieved.[38] Of the two women, it is the unknown *usted* who represents the concept of finality and perfection.

The second structural device, also unusual for Mallea, is the insertion of a novel within the novel. Martín Tregua is working on *The Forty Nights of Juan Argentino* which reminds one strongly of the focus and rhetorical style employed earlier in *History of an Argentine Passion*. A brief selection will establish this relationship. After proclaiming that the land was entrusted to foreign hands, that the country lay stagnant, Martín Tregua goes on to show the need for a spiritual, intellectual, and heroic imagination that would illuminate the darkest corners of the big city. He proceeds to defend a national prototype that is scarcely distinguishable from the models set up by such ultranationalists as Manuel Gálvez or Pedro Orgambide:

Juan Argentino—our man [Professor Burescu] said to me—is exploited by those who sell him out. What becomes important is to look stubbornly everywhere for Juan Argentino. We must set him apart from his exploiters and give him the place he has earned through his misfortunes. Juan Argentino is ignored, unknown, while Juan Inglés, Juan Italiano, Juan Alemán, all these foreign Johns, are the bosses. Juan Argentino is like a child. It is essential, then, to make him into a new man.[39]

Thereupon Martín Tregua becomes inspired to write his *magnum opus*, *The Forty Nights of Juan Argentino*, that would delineate and exult above all the dignity and the nobility of spirit in this symbolic figure that exists as yet in a submerged state: "Juan Argentino is the man who needs to be created by all of us here. He is the new man born from our life blood, from the impotence and frustration of all that belonged to the old generation, and who was born from the best and most valuable assets that formed part of the old order."[40]

The Forty Nights of Juan Argentino obviously constitute a recapitulation of themes found earlier in *History of an Argentine Passion*. Mallea felt the need to restate his unsolved problems in his search for the genuine Argentine inhabitant, and this time establishes the central figure of Martín Tregua to fictionalize what previously was shaped in essaylike form. The Tregua-Mallea axis, then, represents a step beyond the expository prose of the earlier Mallea. Professor Donald L. Shaw focuses on this technical aspect and its relation to the essayistic novel cultivated by members of the Spanish "Generation of '98" when writing: ". . . *La bahía del silencio* belongs to the class of 'discussion fiction' brought into vogue in Spain by the "Generation of '98" and notably Baroja. It may be defined as consisting of biographical or autobiographical novels in which a central character, reflecting the author's preoccupations, faces a series of test situations and carefully selected interlocutors."[41]

In order to create the illusion of a dialogue, a sizeable cast of supporting actors has been assigned the function of issuing essayistic reflections as well as prompting the main character's reactions. As Donald Shaw remarked, looking at the second part of the novel, "Tregua's four main interlocutors in Book II, Ferrier, Atkinson, Anteriello and Scariol, are designed not only to typify the decadence of the intelligentsia in Europe but also to voice attitudes and opinions which throw into relief his continuing spiritual evolution."[42]

While one can easily agree with Professor Shaw that "Tregua is continuously unable to forge for himself a coherent set of vital convictions,"[43] his veneration for the archetypal *usted* allows for a possible *rapprochement* with Mallea's idealized national conscience. Cast in this archetypal role, the mysterious *usted* represents a state of finality and perfection that constitutes a desirable essence according to Max Scheler's definition of a genuine personality. The German philosopher distinguishes between what he calls sham-personality, molded after examples or models, and an essence-personality which feeds on inherent qualities. For Scheler the latter is indispensable to bringing out the genuine potentialities in a person. For Mallea, who read Scheler and quotes him in some of his essays such as *The Sense of Intelligence in the Expression of Our Time*, this genuine potential is inextricably bound to a noble form of self-expression. Like Jean Jacques Rousseau, the Argentine novelist adopts a position of optimism about the human being's "true" nature.[44] If the *usted* figure can sustain the burden of being the image and prototype of Mallea's potential Argentina, he will for once have attained his elusive goal. Unfortunately, she remains but an idealization of Martín Tregua throughout the pages of his overly long confession. However, toward the very end of the third book we find Martín Tregua approaching a state of simplicity and artless nobility that would lead to the discovery of the true self, a self akin to that of the redeeming female. Thus he exclaims: "I have reduced my life to its most elementary forms. I now only associate with very, very simple people. Every day I seem to reach farther inside of me; I am almost in the silent heart of my land."[45] Perhaps Tregua as well as his creator seem to feel that the final step toward finding a personal "Argentine" solution is near.

CHAPTER 4

The National Cycle

I *The Novelist and La gana*

THE transition from *The Bay of Silence* to *All Green Shall Perish* seemed to be an effortless one. Mallea himself stated that both works were written almost simultaneously.[1] But he went on to say that they stood worlds apart, allowing him to test his pen in an entirely different technique. Mallea realized that by working with a stricter form and tighter plot he could gain in dramatic tone. He himself saw the problem as one of "action versus digression" and admitted that "thus I avoided the difficulties that the novelist faces when drifting in a limitless and uncontrollable sea; and there is no doubt that a stricter control of the subject matter helps to produce a result that is artistically speaking superior."[2] Mallea obviously possesses more than enough novelistic acumen to realize that his pursuit of the "personal" novel detracts from the aesthetic unity that most of the critics and readers hoped to find in his works. Yet, he confesses his predilection for such works as *The Bay of Silence*, adding that he felt attracted to its amorphous context, satisfied that "he wrote this book with the love and fervor that goes together with a sort of adolescent rebelliousness in its purest state."[3]

Mallea's "confession" touches upon a cardinal aspect of his work: that of being *un escritor de la gana*, a self-indulgent writer. It is this aspect that has brought about the genuine and repeated criticism of all those who found in his writings an undisciplined projected ego that takes on, chameleonlike, the disguises of the confessional tone, the art or literature lecturer, the fervid essayistic invocation, the Socratic dialogue, or simply the recapitulation of established archetypes. On the other hand, Mallea's novelistic techniques, as witnessed in *The Bay of Silence*, constitute a unique transitional occurrence: a nexus between the "antinovels" found among the

76

writers of the "Generation of '98," be it Unamuno, Baroja, or Azo-rín, and the personal novel of the 1960s, cultivated by a Nathalie Sarraute in France or Guillermo Cabrera Infante in Cuba. It should be added, however, that Mallea's amorphous novels did not stem from a willed process of decomposition or dehumanization in protest at worn-out art forms and bankrupt sociopolitical systems which provided a convenient context for the "bourgeois" novel. In the case of Mallea's amorphous novels we witness the involuntary expansion of his self that moves almost at will, guided by a self-centered spirit. For this reason novels like *All Green Shall Perish* and *Chaves* stand out as sparkling jewels of dramatic intensity, a contrast fully acknowledged by the writer himself.[4]

II All Green Shall Perish

While a number of characters in *The Bay of Silence* have been borrowed from real life, the protagonists of *All Green Shall Perish* are totally invented.[5] However, the novelist took great care to pattern his background after places he visited purposely before picking up his pen, especially those located near Bahía Blanca, his home town. Mallea perhaps realized that it was time to turn away from the milieu of Buenos Aires with its beaten paths and urban characters that appeared so often in his previous works, if he was finally to discover the true nature of Argentina. Thus he begins to feel his way across the land, as silent and often as barren as its inhabitants.

As the novel begins we see and feel a land that is in its forty-fifth day of devastation by a biblical, wrathful drought. The action takes place near Bahía Blanca in the southern part of the enormous Buenos Aires province where empty masses of land foreshadow the austral regions of arid and lifeless Patagonia. The descriptive passages appropriately focus on life-taking images: "hirsute land, skeletonlike trees, the exhausted thread of a clear-water river, an emaciated errant scrawny beef dragging itself to a dried-up stream, sand-filled air, blanched animal bones, calcinated earth. . . ."[6] "The place was like the backyard of Job in its vision of aridness and death";[7] and the preface quoting from Ecclesiastes reminds the reader that an ill wind will bring bad times to man when least expected.

In this setting the two main characters, Nicanor Cruz and his wife Agata, move in ever-tightening circles of silence, rancor, and sterility. After more than fifteen years of failure to produce green pas-

tures, to bear fruit, or to bring forth human life, their relationship is
one of friction, despair, and mutual rejection. Nicanor has become
the symbol of inevitable failure (*fracasado de antemano*) and of negative maleness (*macho sombrío*) after years of struggle with the barren pampas. Agata feels oppressed by layers of sterility and silence.
The daughter of a drunkard Protestant minister who had named her
after the piece of agate that her mother stared at while in the agony
of death, she had hoped to transcend her original state of self-
contained melancholia by marrying Nicanor Cruz. Flashbacks recreate her adolescence in Ingeniero White, a township next to the
port of Bahía Blanca. In this environment—also the world of the
young Mallea—a panorama emerges that is filled with the foreign
voices of English railroad workers, Scandinavian grain dealers,
German inns like the Kaiserhof, docked ships with Anglo-Saxon
names, or the Londres tea room, filled with a correctly dressed and
behaved afternoon crowd, a world in which the pampas and their
inhabitants seem but a complement or an afterthought. But after
marrying Cruz the positive mixture of European vestiges and the
salt-sprayed south Atlantic fades away, and Agata becomes confined
in her tragic isolation and unyielding pride. As critic John A. Crow
stated, "she carried a desert in her womb, a desert in her soul and a
desert in her heart and a desert in her mind: she had been dragged
by that man against her will to his own recesses of darkness and
taciturnity."[8] As her daily routine became a final dispersal of her
vitality (*un aniquilamiento*), she was prompted to wish for a stop to
her tortured existence: "And in the house one could only breathe
hatred, one could only digest hatred. 'My God,' she thought feeling
the dryness in her mouth, 'please put an end to this. I cannot go on
any longer.' "[9] The climax to this unbearable situation comes during
the next winter as Nicanor Cruz lies bedridden, ill with pneumonia
in the midst of outer and inner desolation, almost proud of his
condition that equals one more defeat and failure. In a sudden
instinctive burst of action, Agata tears off her clothes, throws doors
and windows wide open, and collapses on the floor while the icy
Patagonian air sweeps the room. In the morning the *peones* find the
two ice-cold bodies, but Cruz' already wears the stiffness of death.

In the second part of the novel the reader is returned to Bahía
Blanca where Agata has come to retrace the only steps that might
lead to a physical and spiritual renewal. The city, however, appears
enveloped in a spirit of moneymaking and contagious prosperity.

Mallea's style waxes incisively ironic as he describes the townspeople: physicians who came to make money, shrewd lawyers, young accountants in silk shirts, bartering and prosperous members of the International Rotary Club, merchants driving away in their new Buicks or Mercedes Benz, and unmarried girls exchanging "lucrative glances" and parading their personal treasures up and down the main avenues, ready to join in the general prosperity.[10] Onto this scene drifts the lonely figure of Agata Cruz, shell-like and silent, yet waiting for somebody, expecting something as she goes through the daily motions of getting up every morning, appearing at the hotel's dining hall, and sitting in cafés for hours on end. Only after meeting one Ema de Volpe and through her a group of extroverts does Agata begin to enter into the intricate maze of social relationships. Among this group is the lawyer Sotero, dynamic, resolute, gay, and boisterous. Captivated by this whirlwind appearance, Agata with great ease enters into a love affair with the man who is so reminiscent of Carlos Oro, the self-centered hedonist who was the protagonist of "The Rhapsody of the Happy Scoundrel." Although we are never informed about the mental workings of Agata and can only speculate about her feelings, she obviously seems to respond to human warmth and is willing to yield part of herself in her lovemaking to Sotero. In spite of Sotero's meaningless dynamism and his false jovial exterior, he means enough to Agata for her to want to retain him. Always reticent to explore sexual avenues, Mallea confines himself to indicating that "toward the morning hours in Sotero's hotel she refused to get up."[11] Sotero, eager to keep up appearances, discourages her presence and soon finds an excuse to slip away to Buenos Aires. Taking his departure to be the final confirmation of her lonely destiny, Agata falls into a stupor, avoiding all human contact and left with the certainty of her utter desolation. The last scenes of the novel find her solitary figure being pursued by a gang of malicious youngsters, like Orestes fleeing the furies, against the background of the deserted town and the nearby empty countryside.

Filled with biblical allusions applicable to the rural setting, the personality of Nicanor and Agata and their apparently predetermined fate, the novel is steeped in a mood best described as total gloom, relentless pathos, and pessimism based on the predestined nature of the individual. At this point the reader might well ask himself if Agata can hold an appeal as a full-fledged human being

as the possibilities of reaching any kind of personal fulfillment are
blocked from the outset. In the preface to his edition of *All Green
Shall Perish*, Donald Shaw raises several questions connected with
the limited autonomy of thought and action awarded to Agata by her
creator:

If we assemble a collection of the (usually pessimistic) comments about
existence in the abstract which are readily found in *Todo verdor perecerá*, it
is clear that those which can definitely be attributed to Agata and those
more or less obviously inserted by Mallea are identical in tone. It then
becomes hard to resist the conclusion that Mallea both denies Agata ulti-
mate insight and makes her think as if she possessed it, at some risk to
consistency. The reason is not far to seek. To have given Agata real insight
would have obliged Mallea to let her fight her way through solitude to
authentic existence and thus to communication.[12]

It seems appropriate to accept Professor Shaw's statement that
Agata Cruz and Eduardo Mallea form an indivisible totality, a situation that would not surprise the attentive reader of such works as
European Nocturne or *The Bay of Silence*. But by focussing re-
lentlessly on the protagonist and her immediate surroundings, be it
the farmhouse, the land, or the port city, Mallea has happily elimi-
nated the ballast of his earlier commentaries, essayistic discussions
on other subjects extraneous to the traditional novel. Although
Agata Cruz conveys the monotony of a one-dimensional being, her
condition becomes effectively dramatized in terms of human suffering and a quasi-mystical experience. Professor Gillessen did well to
compare Agata's frame of mind to the mental state of the Spanish
mystic San Juan de la Cruz, the author of *Dark Night of the Soul*
(*Noche oscura en el alma*).[13] Removed from the habitual cosmopolitan scene and divested of his favorite intellectualizing protagonists,
Mallea's work has gained greatly in dramatic intensity and descriptive powers. In spite of the fact that the land—the true Argentina for
Mallea—lies barren and looms inhospitable, its essential powers and
quiet grandeur filter through the surface of desolation.

III   The Eagles

Talking about his next novel, *The Eagles (Las águilas)*, which
appeared in 1943, Mallea stated that this work was to form part of a
trilogy.[14] The second volume, *The Tower (La torre)*, did indeed
appear a few years later, whereas the third one, which was to finish

the history of the Ricarte family and to be entitled *The Tempest*, has not yet appeared. Thinking back about the genesis of this trilogy, the author claimed that "the idea of the triptych occurred to me suddenly when a friend of mine once told me the story of a farm he had purchased fully realizing that he might never be able to meet his financial obligations. Although the anecdote has all but faded from my memory, in its place I invented the idea of presenting a tract of land and its manor that slowly devour its owner."[15]

Without cultivating a genetic kind of criticism, it is possible to go beyond this author's autobiographical account and evaluate the organic framework created in good measure by subconscious forces. The themes developed in *The Eagles* outdistance by far the level of the original anecdote. The late Argentine critic Luis Emilio Soto, for instance, points at such themes as the rise and fall of an upper-class family, the moral decay of Argentina's landed gentry, and the formation of an Argentine class spirit.[16] Soto takes a close look at the three generations of Ricartes that move through the pages of this novel and notices the elaboration of the fortunes and misfortunes that constitutes a classical family cycle. It was typical at the turn of the century for the hard-working immigrant from Spain, Italy, or Ireland to "make America" and amass a fortune which then was automatically equated with land, grain, and cattle. Leon Ricarte, unperturbed pioneer, conquers the land almost by chance, taking it as something that was waiting to be taken by the rightful newcomer. Only slowly did he learn that owning land meant power, prestige, and acceptance by those who had set the tone and made the laws in a country still in search of its identity. How little the Spanish immigrant Leon Ricarte appreciated this virgin land became clear when he ordered the construction of Las Aguilas, a mansion representing a conglomerate of European traditions and illusions, planted in the midst of the fleeting pampas. Immense, pompous, and wistful, Las Aguilas was incongruent, vainly upholding a distorted European legacy in the heart of Mallea's "ethical land."

Leon Ricarte dies and his only heir, Román Ricarte, is destined to dissipate the family fortune. Weak in disposition he follows the dicta of society without questioning any of its values. Passionless and indecisive he plays the prescribed roles of young man about town, country squire, and eligible bachelor. He obtains a law degree although he does not plan to practice his profession, he drops a girl who is socially unacceptable to his peers, and he marries the daughter of an impoverished but prominent *criollo* family. From then on his dramatic movements are furnished by quarrels with his wife and daughters, socially overambitious and overly frivolous in the worst tradition of *fin de siècle* high society. The endless lavish spending on the part of Emilia Ricarte and her daughters bring about financial crises that force Ramón Ricarte to sell land in order to purchase a myriad of artifacts that fill their town house. Condemned to preside over the liquidation of his patrimony, Ramón Ricarte's hopes and illusions are projected toward his only son Roberto.

Following in his father's footsteps in becoming a lawyer, Roberto leaves the parental mansion in order to associate with some of his discontented fellow students and pronounce himself in favor of change. However, as happened in *The Bay of Silence*, neither he nor his friends are inclined to produce more than empty phrases like "I am against an order based on dead conscience" or "they poison the country."[17] As an indictment, such criticism falls short of establishing concrete plans of action; yet, the indictment is there embodied by a downward cycle ending in decay and ruin. For Luis Emilio Soto it becomes a matter of the sons of the landed gentry reacting to their being disinherited and trying to discover an ideology suitable to echo their plight.[18]

But Mallea actually does not define the context in which this decay takes place. Are we, for instance, to comprehend the creation of the great agrarian fortunes as desirable socially and morally? Ezequiel Martínez Estrada, Mallea's influential contemporary, would have condemned León Ricarte's pioneering efforts as a rapacious bit of plundering, involving the Saint Simonist adage that property equaled theft. The Argentine writer H. A. Murena who continued Martínez Estrada's probing into the foundation of America's destiny sees the worst elements of the Old World invading the placidity of America and converting it into a second Paradise Lost.[19] The worst, in Murena's terms, came to the New World blinded by the myth of Eldorado ready to pick up the gold or snatch it from their neighbors. In *The Eagles* we find a wholesale condemnation of a frivolous and materialistic way of life whose artificiality and false values stand out clearly after the first few pages. In fact, Emilia Islas, her precious daughters, and their entourage are but a carbon copy of Madame de Rague standing in her salon crammed with expensive artifacts in *Fiesta in November*, and the reader tires of these figures long before the author disposes of them. Mallea then makes his point early enough in the novel. But what about their counterpart, what of the spiritual life? Here Mallea comes up against his old nemesis: the elusive sources of spiritual power that go into making up his genuine Argentina. Of all the available references concerning the virtues of the genuine Argentine spirit the following passage seems the most representative; in fact, it is strongly reminiscent of the portrait of the ideal Argentine way of life established in *History of an Argentine Passion* and of a vision shared by Mallea's father.

In those years [1895 and onward] Buenos Aires was far from being the city it is today when its size can easily account for its spiritual dissolution. Then it still conserved the pure *criollo* way of life that subsequent avalanches of immigrants have dissolved into a characterless multitude. In those days Buenos Aires represented a healthy colonial capital still dominated by the past . . . with only a handful of modern buildings that had more than one floor smack between these pretty and plain homes, aristocratic-looking with their interior patios and corridors. General education was still being administered according to principles that had become familiar because of the traditions they represented and university studies were inspired by a paternalistic if not patriarchal system. The students were usually sons of known families from the city or the provinces; and it was difficult to find a name that had no background. Román [Ricarte] got to know the professors who had a national reputation as public figures and who treated their pupils like relatives or sons. Teaching was a moral process then, and pedagogy a form of ethics. This process might have been unscientific but the end result, as far as morality went, was positive.[20]

This composite picture of the Argentine *Belle Epoche* contains ample evidence of Mallea's predilection and judgment concerning aesthetics, upbringing, and morality. Here one could easily ask the question: was an old-fashioned sense of aesthetics, pedagogy, and ethics enough to qualify as the basis for the genuine expression of the Argentine spirit? Martínez Estrada and Murena would have hardly thought so. True spirituality hardly springs from pedigree, land deeds, or Senecan morality.

The novel ends with an episode apparently unrelated to its plot or structure. An unknown peon from a neighboring *estancia*, named Caledonio, is fatally injured as he falls from his horse. When asked whether he should be brought into Las Aguilas, Ramón Ricarte simply replies: "What for? Out here is his land and his air."[21] Once

again, Mallea approaches the land and its inhabitant as if searching
for a communion that cannot begin to take place through his main
characters and what they represent.

IV *Interlude*

In 1943 the political developments in Argentina took an alarming
turn. The generals who had toppled the weak rightwing government
of Dr. Ramón Castillo succeeded each other without being able to
lead the country onto a path of civic responsibility or socioeconomic
reforms that were badly overdue in a nation filled with a literate and
syndicalist-minded electorate. It fell upon Colonel Juan Domingo
Perón to seize the opportunity to proclaim himself champion of the
descamisados—the shirtless ones who felt exploited by their
laissez-faire minded captains of industry and neglected by the conservative politicians—and establish a populist autocracy in which
the landowner, the bourgeois professional, and the dissenting intellectual became the enemy of the people. The Perón era and its
preamble extend across the midcentury mark, from 1943 till 1955
when a new army uprising brought about the fall of this most singular regime that combined in strange ways political demagoguery,
neofascist strains, and a catastrophic economic policy based on
populist sympathies. While the celebrated couple, Juan and Evita
Perón, produced the most unique sociopolitical rule that Argentina
or for that matter any Latin American country was to experience, its
effects on the national literary scene were equally unique.

Due to the overwhelming popularity of the Perón regime among
the working class—after all the great majority of the population—
the intellectual or writer who had previously engaged in the proverbial class struggle by siding with the working man or socialist causes
(such as the early Boedo group) found himself suddenly confronted
with the painful decision of either turning his back on the toiling
masses or agreeing with Perón's demagoguery and venal administra-
tive practices. The net result was an almost absolute silence. The
literary establishment to which Mallea belonged continued to cultivate its own artistic garden while throwing furtive glances at the
national situation and continuing its association with the rather
aristocratic-minded elite. Some of its most prominent members
began to feel the heavy hand of Perón's power; thus Jorge Luis
Borges, who had previously made a modest living by working in a
public library, was appointed inspector of chicken coops, and oligar-

chic Victoria Ocampo, the millionairess-patron of *Sur* and its entourage, was arrested, fingerprinted, and jailed. Mallea continued
to direct the "Literary Supplement" of *La Nación*, painfully aware
that any day the newspaper might become nationalized by its
working-class critics.

Mallea, who prior to the Perón era had categorically rejected such
avenues as social realism or political commentary in his writings,
would obviously continue to elaborate themes and symbols that had
preoccupied and inspired him earlier. Of all the major writers in
Argentina during this period, only Martínez Estrada ventured an
inquiry into the sociopolitical state of affairs with a short essay called
What Is That? (*¿Qué es eso?*) At any rate, the next two works
produced by Mallea denote an introspection that could easily be
taken for a withdrawal into his personal essence. *Surrounded by
Dreams (Rodeada está de sueño)* and its sequel *The Return (El
retorno)* came out in 1944 and 1946 respectively. In his somewhat
autobiographical work, *The Inner War*, Mallea refers to these two
volumes by the subtitle "Poetic Memoirs of an Unknown Person"
and indicates that they represent an attempt to portray what he calls
"the well educated soul" (*alma bien educada*). What predominates
in these two works is a highly subjective mood that allows the author
to record remembrances of things past, especially those related to
his childhood, and to do it in an effortless way, since he did not have
to fictionalize his remembrances and illusions. The oneiric element
combined with a poetic prose style gives these two books a hermetic
quality that charms the reader without pretending to be a major
fictional effort.

The year 1946 also saw the publication of Mallea's three short
novels in one volume, "The Bond" ("El Vínculo"), "The Rembrandt
Family" (Los Rembrandt"), and "Cernobbio's Rose" ("La rosa de
Cernobbio"). These *nouvelles* seem to elaborate events and impressions that reach back into the novelist's earlier life; certainly "The
Rembrandt Family" dates back to the Olympic Games held in
Amsterdam in 1928 which young Mallea attended as a correspondent for *La Nación*. Actually none of these three short works have
drawn the attention of the critics, and it might be well to speculate
that Mallea just felt compelled to exhaust earlier impressions before
exploring new themes and topics. He soon became busy with the
sequel to *The Eagles*, finishing *The Tower (La torre)* in 1947 while
simultaneously working on *The Enemies of the Soul (Los enemigos*

del alma). The latter appeared in 1950 while *The Tower* was published in 1951.

V   The Enemies of the Soul

Talking about the genesis of *The Enemies of the Soul,* Mallea
states that long ago his brother had interested him with a tale about
a house in their native Bahía Blanca where two old maids tried to
stop their brother from returning late from his nightly escapades by
blocking the entrance with furniture.[22] Given this nucleus, Mallea
quickly enlarged its scope to spin a tale of opposing symbols that for
the critic Enrique González Lanuza represent diabolic and angelic
forces fighting in a renewed battle of the spirit and the flesh.[23] The
novel appears to have been reeled off the author's mind with accustomed clarity and speed. Mallea himself stated the following:

> While I wrote this novel, I was surprised that the characters, the
> background, and the episodes came to me visually. I told myself, "Why do I
> write all this down in such a slow fashion when in reality it should be
> captured with the aid of a movie camera?" . . . It seemed that the novel was
> being dictated to me, that is how strongly I experienced the characters,
> destinies, conflicts, or happenings. . . . In other works, like in *All Green
> Shall Perish,* a poetic exultation had carried me along. In *The Bay of Silence*
> a youthful yearning for love, tenderness, pity, justice, and companionship
> dominated. But in *The Enemies of the Soul,* it was a sort of visual exultation
> that took hold of me.[24]

Although definitely entrenched in the cosmopolitan life of the
Argentine capital, Mallea makes a spiritual pilgrimage to his native
Bahía Blanca for *The Enemies of the Soul.* The primary result of "the
return of the native" was an overpowering immersion in the local
milieu set this time in the 1930s. The descriptive element clearly
dominates every facet of the novel. Through a multitude of secondary characters, the port city springs to life, from the seagoing men
to the young clerks in silk shirts eagerly discussing the local supply
of women, from the self-righteous matrons to the older lawyers and
grain merchants dining in an all-male atmosphere. Mallea truly ex-
cels in establishing a full-blown version of life in his hometown,
making it so tangible and direct that the reader can feel the wintry
blasts blowing the sand from the desolate dunes into the well-heated
homes of the good citizen, ride along with the fiacre or taxi
through the foggy streets of the town at dusk, and follow the sailors

or young bachelors to the labyrinth of narrow streets where reddish lights announce the promise of contrived pleasures. However, the general *Zeitgeist* indicates rather a *fin-de-siècle* mood than a sprawling city on the eve of World War II. In large measure this mood becomes intensified by a choice of vocabulary and phrases that conjure up an earlier period. Mallea himself became aware of this practice and went on to defend it with his accustomed vehemence.

Some have reproached me for using in places throughout the novel difficult or esoteric terminology. The reason for this usage is very simple. On one hand . . . I wanted to endow the book with elements that would make it richer, more valuable. . . . On the other hand I used words like *hético* instead of tubercular or *estantigua* for strange appearance because my family comes from the provinces—my father had been born in San Juan and as a child I heard my aunts and grandmother use a rustic vocabulary—and thus these and similar terms were common and familiar to me. It is—or should be—common knowledge that in our provinces the familiar expressions have been full of nuances and a richness filled with native meanings that show originality as well as a national spirit, whereas in Buenos Aires precisely the opposite occurred due to an immigration that has denaturalized and obscured our language.[25]

Perhaps the evocation of a city and its life blood that carries the author back to the days of his adolescence has been instrumental in producing a concurrent linguistic tone. We also find autobiographical indicators such as the mentioning of the Australian headmistress who ran the English grammar school in Bahía Blanca to which Mallea refers in the reminiscences contained in *History of an Argentine Passion*.[26]

Against the background of his Bahía Blanca, Mallea has the five protagonists divided into two groups: the three descendants of José Guillén and Ortigosa and wife. All five become soon recognizable as true enemies of the spiritual realm. José Guillén's offspring live in Villa Rita, the mansion built by their father, a place befitting their mood. Musty and reeking of staleness and humidity, the dwelling, dilapidated and gloomy, stands forlorn amid the frequent fog and drizzle drifting over from the ever-present ocean. The three inhabitants show themselves to be prisoners of the past and victims of the present, overpowered by the gloomy setting and daily friction. Misanthropic and vain, their progenitor had kept his beautiful wife jealously away from the worldly pleasures and had seen his love turn

into a brutalizing possessiveness. The three children were conceived as an act of self-affirmation and male dominance over the
stoic passivity of the wife. Until the death of José Guillén, the three
children lived and recreated the vivid feeling of hatred and misan-
thropy that filled Villa Rita. After the parents' disappearance the
three evolved into parallel entities tragically marked by this past.
Mario, drawn in the most vivid colors, lusts after pleasure; hungry
for sensations, he descends daily onto the city to look for a prey, a
victim, a moment of intrigue or excitement, be it in the form of a
card game, a new romance, a shady business deal, or a night of
debauchery. His sister Cora also makes daily sorties onto the town.
More hermetic than Mario, she nevertheless is avid for pleasure and
excitement that she tracks down with deliberate voluptuousness and
a display of a terrible *desgana total.* She exhibits an abysmal indifference to everything but a latent hedonism that is reborn each noon
when she gets up to ponder the new day and its gratifying prospects.
Debora, the oldest, appears on the surface to be the opposite of her
brother and sister: hermetic, obstinately antisocial, and excessively
puritanical, she embodies a total negation of life. Condemned to
stew in her own bitter juices, she can only experience vicariously
the imagined pleasures of her brother and sister, which allows her to
both condemn and be condemned. All three, however, share the
malaise engendered by their father; all three go through life sup-
pressing the smallest evidence of spirituality. When Luis Ortigosa
and his wife move to Bahía Blanca, Mario uses his Dorian Grey-like
charms in an attempt to seduce Consuelo Ortigosa, while Cora flirts
with Consuelo's husband. The Ortigosas form a strange counterpart
to the inhabitants of Villa Rita. Consuelo had married Ortigosa to
save her father; thereafter she retreated into a world of her own,
never forgiving her husband a Platonic interest in a young girl
whose artistic ambitions he shared. Consuelo's lethargy and Luis'
indifference create a state of passivity that invites the advances of
Mario and Cora. When Debora suspects the intimate relations
among the four, her suppressed anguish and resentment break wide
open. She writes anonymous letters to the Ortigosas, but they fail to
arouse the interest of either spouse. She then decides to leave Villa
Rita, but soon realizes that Mario and Cora would be only too
pleased by her absence. Debora now faces a final decision, namely,
to break her bondage and leave or to preside over the collective
destruction of the Guillén family. Her poisoned mind does not allow

her to be generous. She ignites the livingroom curtains and perishes in the flames next to her brother and sister. Only the statue of the Apollo of Belvedere, so admired by Mario, remains unscathed. In an open letter to Mallea, the Argentine essayist and critic Enrique González Lanuza admonishes the novelist, saying that as an incarnation of the diabolical element, Debora falls short of symbolizing evil because "she is only evil in a human way, too human really, and as such does not quite accomplish what she was meant to do."[27] In his reply to González Lanuza, Mallea quite rightfully points out that it was never his intention to deal with allegorical figures but rather complex human beings who possess a wide range of contradictory emotions.[28] Debora's acts are indeed guided by an evil spirit, but one born out of a sterile past that determines her character, thoughts, and behavior. In this sense she simply shares a dismal past with Mario and Cora, a fate that bears closer resemblance to the characters in Jean Paul Sartre's *No Exit* than the demons in Dante's *Inferno*. Mallea's *Weltanschauung* does not rely on medieval representations, and the trinity of devil–flesh–worldliness is not woven into the tapestry of his prose. Rather, the original sin of Debora as well as of the other protagonists of this novel stems from being predetermined, condemned to a process of sterility and resentment against humanity. Frustrated in their awareness of not being able to reach out from the confines of their own shell, they have turned enemies of humanity and scorned the spiritual life.

Before publishing *The Enemies of the Soul*, Mallea had already written the second volume of the proposed trilogy that began with *The Eagles*. This volume, entitled *The Tower*, appeared in 1951. As a continuation of the fortunes and misfortunes of the Ricarte family, Mallea now features the grandson of León Ricarte, immigrant founder of the dynasty. Roberto Ricarte appears to combine the virtues and defects of the two previous generations. He feels swayed by the spirit of the land and its regenerative force, yet he spends most of his time in Buenos Aires where a life of social interchange and facile camaraderie with former schoolmates or his father's acquaintances allows for such attractive possibilities as discussing the meaning of art or the course of Argentine history. In the background we find the Ricarte family: Roberto's father Ramón, his wife Emilia Islas, daughters, and respective sons-in-law. None of them have changed much since we saw them last in *The Eagles*. Dr. Ramón Ricarte parades his genteel mien and shabby gentility through the

different book stores of the capital and can be found reading such
unbelievable relics as Julius Caesar's *De Bellum Gallicum;* and his
wife continues to mix with the cream of society, holding soirees,
exchanging bon mots and chastising her inert husband when he fails
to bring home a case of Lacrima Christi for an impending party.

The attentive reader of Mallea's novels recognizes these characters since they have appeared in a good number of his previous
works. Roberto Ricarte could be Adrian in *European Nocturne* or
Martín Tregua in *The Bay of Silence*, searching for a meaning to life
while spending his daily unencumbered hours in endless talks in
one café or another, drinking and eating his way through the ever
recurring perimeter of downtown Buenos Aires and the adjacent
Barrio Norte, yearning for fulfillment and turning toward the silent,
fertile land. Even Calila Montes, Roberto Ricarte's female companion, has not changed since the days and ways of Cristiana Ruiz in
The City Next to the Motionless River. She is Mallea's eternal
female, dressed in a tailored suit, aristocratic, languid, and aloof,
confronting an evasive lover on a silent nocturnal street or amid the
impeccable decor of a town house. The Mallean reader is also used
by now to dialogues studded with celebrities like Baudelaire,
Freud, Bach, or Kant and laced with tea, cognac, or wine. Luis
Emilio Soto sums up the tone of the novel by writing: "It is well
known that Mallea has the tendency of creating a sustained pathetic
novel in which his characters move around aimlessly, love, suffer,
and above all indulge in obstinate monologues, filled with a desperate dissatisfaction. No ray of happiness or humor ever reaches these
minds wrapped in abstractions, prisoners of incertitudes and boundless malcontent."[29] Stylistically, a number of Mallea's favorite terms
reappear with accustomed frequency underlining the personality of
the protagonists; we find words like languor (*dejadez*), fatigue (*can-
sancio*), indifference (*indiferencia*), inertia (*inercia*), fatuous (*fatuo*),
unwillingness (*desgano*), and lassitude (*lasitud*).

Structurally the novel is divided into three segments of which the
first and the last take place in Las Aguilas, the magnificent ruin built
by the grandfather and now the sole remaining piece of property of
the Ricarte family. Roberto Ricarte, now thirty-eight, makes one of
his infrequent appearances at the somber and dilapidated mansion
where the loyal servant couple Juan and Gracia Mota takes solicitous
care of him. The rustic scene comes alive through a somewhat

idealized description of the land and even the adjacent small town of Vallares, emanating a desirable quotient of tradition, stability, order, and continuity. Roberto Ricarte, for the first time in his life, seems to be fully aware that "the mother earth stretched out endlessly, giving birth to green food."[30] He now reacts accordingly.

> What love did he feel for all this. A love that preceded him and would live on after he would be buried in the land. He felt the need for confession, clarity, cleansing, and candor, all of which ought to be like the fountainhead of his country, deeply grounded in the heart of the soil . . . in a sort of communion that went much further than the ties to his own blood. . . . He wanted to be shouting into the wind freeing his soul of all that was old and musty, saying things that he had never dared to say, prisoner of his old self and buried in conventionalism.[31]

At this point Mallea contrasts the regenerative powers of the land with the noxious influence of the city. Roberto Ricarte looks at the alternatives and tells himself: "Yet, what harsh, unpleasant life awaited him in the city to which he would return in a few days, and how little of this loyal and solemn feeling of solidarity would he be able to take along?"[32]

Overly long and repetitious, the second division of the novel serves to intensify this contrast. The protagonist, his friends and acquaintances all participate in the bourgeois routine so typical of Mallea's urban portrayals, always conversing, analyzing, protesting, endlessly eating and drinking, and never exercising a known profession (Roberto Ricarte does try one single case in court which he promptly loses). When the family finances are hopelessly exhausted, Roberto musters enough determination to move the family to Las Aguilas where he and Juan Mota are going to farm some leased land.

In the final part we find the Ricarte family permanently exposed to the magnetic pull of the land; and Roberto yields his inner reality to the natural grandeur surrounding him now. Given the usual frustration of Mallea's tormented heroes, the protagonist of *The Tower* has come closer to a solution than his predecessors. Yet, how does playing the country squire create a spiritual identification with the soil? Juan Mota will do the actual toiling on the land and treat Roberto with a deference born out of a master-servant relationship. Once again, Luis Emilio Soto with his accustomed critical acumen and impeccable logic hits the right note when remarking:

Does Roberto succeed in having his family accept the invigorating ways of rustic life? Don't they actually continue to recreate an existence based on summer visits made to Las Aguilas totally divorced from the meaningful ties to the land and spiritual transformation envisioned by Roberto? The moral cleansing of such sins as social interaction and frivolities and all the coming and going of big-city life, is it not a new pious delusion? . . . Only by virtue of this delusion can Roberto believe that he found a way to solve his crisis. . . .[33]

VI   Chaves

In the preface to *The Tower*, the author talks about the third volume of the proposed trilogy, *The Tempest (La tempestad)*, in which action (presumably that of the protagonist Roberto Ricarte) will bring about the solution of the problems developed in the previous volumes. This ambition remains unfulfilled up to now, but Mallea worked on another novel that appeared in 1953 and that was generally judged to be one of his very best efforts.

There are actually some very good technical reasons for the success of *Chaves:* the author left out all elements that might detract from the linear presentation of a human failure. Gone are the endless discussions on art, literature, history, or philosophy; gone also the repetitious descriptions of bourgeois behavior and milieu; and gone are the morose soliloquies by protagonists whose main occupation consists of eating, drinking, walking, and talking. As a result of the reduced number of pages—perhaps one-fourth of the average work of Mallea—the novel gains in dramatic quality and leaves an emotional impact that could hardly be achieved in a much more diffused structure.

The brief introductory chapters establish Chaves as an allegorical figure: silent, grave, sure of himself, wrapped in anonymity, he provokes a negative reaction among his fellow workers at the sawmill lost in the southwestern mountains of Argentina. Chaves offends by refusing to enter the rules of the shallow world of petty thoughts and expressions held to be important by those who cannot see beyond this pettiness. Yet, his position does not stem from any intellectual reasoning or discovery. Chaves is a simple man. In flashbacks we become aware of his make-up: "hard and dark, a veritable sculptured pole made from wood, hair like coal, burning unblinking eyes, a rigid mouth defiant and aloof, always shut except when open in astonishment."[34] Born and raised in Bahía Blanca by an authoritarian father—a close resemblance to the author's background—he aimlessly lets himself be absorbed by the natural habitat made up of the leaden ocean, the barren dunes, and the windswept streets, growing up without a competitive spirit or worldly ambitions. His world seemed an end and not a means. Only upon meeting Pura, his life's companion, will he consent to apply shabby means to reach a nobler goal. As a married couple, Chaves and Pura live for two years in a desolate place on the ocean where he begins to invent words and phrases to fill the void in their uncomfortable rented room, as if searching for the magic that could transform their drab reality. Chaves, ironically, tried to make a living by selling beach lots, feverishly attempting to conjure up the magic that lies dormant in the spoken word, even though he was aware of misusing this power. A daughter is born and dies at the age of four, leaving Chaves with a most bitter defeat. He goes on mechanically selling useless pieces of sand. "He returned home, late in the evening, his throat dry and his heart filled with hatred. Deep in his soul he resented his fraudulent occupation . . . and sometimes he felt like rushing out into the street to shout out this hatred and the feeling of impotence that were gnawing at his insides."[35] After a while Chaves and Pura take to exploring the country, from the hills of Córdoba to the mountains of Tucumán, finally settling in a nondescript town that represents a typical provincial mood. For a few years they enjoy a relatively stable and relaxed existence, but then Pura suffers an attack of typhoid fever and dies while Chaves in desperation tries to find a cure. One last time he appeals to the spoken word, fervently trying to deter time and fate, hopelessly addressing those who did not comprehend: "He spoke, more deliriously than she, conjuring up an eloquence that represented his entire life, a life that amounted to nothing or almost nothing."[36] As Pura lies dying, Chaves "filled the night with words," eloquent for the last time.[37] His defeat is final; and the peons at the sawmill will see a man who has experienced the failure of mankind's most powerful instrument: the word. As H. A. Murena says in his outstanding study of the novel, "Chaves truly no longer sees the world of man, he sees beyond it."[38]

Having left behind the triviality of endeavor, he must suffer the consequences. Nobody can show himself to be impervious to what is dear to others without paying the penalty of incurring the wrath of the many. Chaves does not appear in the guise of a Christ figure; his spiritual companion would be rather an existentialist antihero like Mersault in Camus' celebrated *L'Etranger*. Both Chaves and Mersault fail to react *properly* to the elaborate social interactions so dear to the social animal in man, and both pay a high price by taking refuge in a dignified hermeticism. Mersault, totally alone, accuses a false humanity that is eagerly awaiting his execution. Chaves, after being rescued by the sawmill's foreman from an attack by his fellow workers, simply utters one syllable to the latter's plea to forego his isolation and talk to the others: "no."

For H. A. Murena, Chaves represents a most Argentine essence and he writes: "In my mind Chaves appears to be an archetype that contains the most outstanding traits of our young spirit."[39] If so, Mallea has been able to isolate a national essence and make it come alive amid most frightening reality: that of man's isolation, a condition that paradoxically serves as a cornerstone of our social edifice, harboring modern society. *Chaves* then looms as a modern tragedy in which the hero acts out of a deep sense of futility while attempting to establish a bridge to other human beings. Mallea establishes the defeat of his protagonist on two levels: the failure of language and the failure of reaching a spiritual rapport even with those he loves most. If there were any doubts that Mallea could be properly included among the ranks of those who pass for the representatives of the modern novel in Latin America, *Chaves* has dispelled them.

VII   The Waiting Room

In *The Inner War* Mallea says of his next novel, *The Waiting Room (La sala de espera)* which also appeared in 1953, that it highlights "a number of intimate conflicts without an apparent solution caught in the most critical moment in which the respective agonist is in the process of waiting or hoping."[40] Thus it is understandable that Mallea should preface the novel with André Gide's statement about Spanish being such a beautiful language because it uses one verb to express the dual act of waiting and hoping.

The novel features seven protagonists and the structure confines them to a desolate waiting room in a small railroad station in the middle of the pampas where they take turns telling their story. There is not the slightest interaction among them; and their mere presence is a pretext to have the author approach them one by one and present their narration in the first person singular. Since Mallea's traditional style permeates all of the narratives, one can easily

detect his idiosyncrasies throughout the different episodes. A similar point of view is held by critic Vicente Barbieri, who maintains
that "Eduardo Mallea has succeeded in this novel—the best within
his vast writings—to have each of the protagonists be himself while
at the same time in some mysterious way being all of them rolled
into one."[41] The seven passengers awaiting an overdue train share a
similarity of expression, look for the precise word, the right simile,
and the learned metaphor; yet they do possess a life of their own.
They share nothing else but the awareness that they must see to it
that their individual destiny should be fulfilled.

The first passenger, one Juan Cormorán, is traveling in search of
his sister. Brought up to achieve material success, he married the
daughter of a wealthy landowner and set out to multiply his dowry,
blind to the spiritual needs of others. When his sister wants to marry
a simple cowhand, Juan Cormorán and his father prevent the marriage and keep her forcibly at home until the father dies. The sister
disappears and Juan continues to pursue his self-made goal until he
discovers that his wife, another of his required possessions, has
sought refuge in the love of a humble fisherman. After an agonizing
look into his past, he begins to feel an urge to become reunited with
his sister, this time in spirit as well as in body.

Violeta Méndez, the second traveler, left a humble and monotonous marital relation in a small town in order to pursue romance and
excitement in the capital. But after a series of lovers and meaningless relationships, she is left with the realization that the main satis-
faction and even pleasure in life can be derived from self-sacrifice, a
theme dear to her creator. Thus she sits in the waiting room ready to
take the night train back to the man whose lonely existence she will
share again.

The next narrator, called Tomás Botón, is the only one of the
seven who moves, ever so obliquely, within the framework of
Peronist Argentina. Mallea here approaches the climate created by
this sociopolitical phenomenon by having the protagonist exclaim:
"Through each door filtered the feeling of great terror. Peacefulness
was substituted by alertness. People trembled with each ringing of
the doorbell."[42] Sensing that political pressure and social conformity
was beginning to corrode and subvert his inner self, Tomás Botón
decided to travel to the heart of the country in order to save himself
from further contamination. As he states, "I want to save what is
important in me, what I really am, my inner voice."[43] Saving his

essence, then, takes precedence over a direct confrontation with the antagonistic forces gripping the nation.

In the following episode we find a reworking of the theme exploited successfully by Unamuno in *Abel Sánchez*, namely the confrontation of two opposing personalities that paradoxically complement each other. Francisco Díaz and his former schoolmate Claudio Murillo share a mutual envy as well as a deep feeling of insecurity that turns into self-hatred and, consequently, a deep resentment against the qualities that appear concentrated in the other person. Thus Francisco Díaz envies Claudio Murillo his elegant cynicism, his debonair mien, and a physician's knowledge, while the latter begrudges Díaz his success as a creative artist, as a playwright. Only after the death of his wife and the failure of his latest play does Díaz provoke a climax in his situation vis-à-vis his alter ego. After an attempt to kill Murillo he disappears from the capital. He begins to travel restlessly hoping to find the complement that would allow him to produce the *magnum opus* that he could not achieve while only an incomplete person.

The last three episodes are short. Of these, the intermediate one clearly stands out. It is the tragic story of Isolina Navarro, a woman who has sacrificed the whole range of human emotions to a rigid formula that was meant to keep her in a state of false pride, haughtiness, and "acid virginity" and make her violently reject the few suitors that might have presented her with the opportunity of giving of herself and of experiencing the capacity of being generous, of loving. Instead she becomes a sixty-year-old spinster who suddenly falls prey to nature's revenge. Thus we see her as a grotesque harpy, covered with cosmetics, wigs, and outlandish clothes, pursuing younger men and running blindly after life. In her pathetic condition, waiting for a train that would allow her to catch up with life, she is the most pitiable of all the people in the waiting room.

As stated at the beginning, what unites the seven personages in this nocturnal scene is the element of hope. However, it becomes quite clear that for the Isolina Navarros their chasing after a hope has reached a point of no return. Even for the others the promise of a happier future seems problematical at best. The strength of these seven independent narratives lies actually in the cathartic effect upon the reader; the characters' weaknesses, foibles, or crimes committed against themselves, others, and the forces of life fill the reader with apprehension and pity.

VIII   Simbad

As the Perón era moved into its final years, the pressure to conform to its ideology and the need to pay at least lip service to its programs or goals became a stark reality. As a writer and an intellectual who has always abhorred the imposition of ideas or norms on others, Mallea throws a retrospective glance onto his situation during the early 1950s.

In periods of dictatorship free men live in prison even if they are not physically placed in one. They are forced to fall back upon themselves since they are not allowed to express their opinion; and without spontaneous communication their moral health declines. Although I escaped being imprisoned between the years 1943 and 1955, I was not free either, since I only could furtively express what my genuine thoughts were. I continued working for the independent newspaper *La Nación* that was constantly threatened with being burned down or closed. Outside of this activity I could only find pleasure in the monastic atmosphere of my home, and even here I was always listening to the doorbell ringing which might have meant that someone was coming to take me away. My only other outlet was to go some afternoons to literary meetings held at the Argentine Association of English Culture where I was privileged to hear free writers coming from free nations talking about works conceived in a free climate, beautiful as freedom itself.[44]

Few indeed were the writers, artists, or intellectuals who could reach a *modus vivendi* with Peronist ideology and political practices. The Argentine writer was firmly rooted in middle- and upper-middle-class values and traditions that characterize such an important segment of Argentine and especially *porteño* society. Populism thus found few echoes amid the Argentine writers, not only among those belonging to the bourgeois group made up of people like Adolfo Bioy Casares, Silvina Bullrich, or Manuel Mujica Lainez but also among the members or descendants of the Boedo group, like Leonidas Barletta or David Viñas, whose sympathies had been for the proletariat. Besides Mallea, the country's foremost prose writers, Jorge Luis Borges, Julio Cortázar, and Ernesto Sábato, cultivated a prose that seldom touched upon sociopolitical realities, although Cortázar and Sábato have demonstrated an affinity for the populist psyche in recent times.
    Although a climate of duress and coercion is obviously detrimental to the writer who is bent on exercising his profession in a genuine

manner, some options of self-expression remain open. Borges himself said that unfavorable conditions such as censorship or intimida-
tion have prompted many a great writer to find an adequate form to
channel his genius, and he cited such examples as Quevedo, Voltaire, and Cela. Mallea himself felt inspired to create a work that
would in its own inimitable way symbolize the ideal of a free individual in a free society. He stated on this subject:

I had the idea of fashioning a novel that would represent a wide world in
which I could move freely to be stimulated and comforted at the same time.
Thus I conceived the novel *Simbad* as equaling a vast free world. . . . Every afternoon from 3 to 8 o'clock I went to work at *La Nación* since I was
editor of the "Literary Supplement." I dedicated my mornings and at times
late evenings to *Simbad*. I felt fascinated by the scope of the work, the
vastness of its temporal flow. I was creating a vast world at the time when a
local world was reducing and oppressing me. My liberty consisted of my
daily meeting with the passage that was to be created. Besides, the central
aspect of this novel fascinated and entertained me. It brought about an
emotional reaction on my part that has been unequaled in my writing. In
fact, I visualized each scene and experienced the characters as being made
of flesh and blood; the whole thing moved me very much.[45]

Taking refuge in the very world he was able to create, Mallea
expands his "inner freedom" into a period of some fifty-five years,
equaling the life span of the author, and consuming almost seven
hundred and fifty pages. Conceived as an *Entwicklungsroman* in the
style of Goethe's *Wilhelm Meister*, the novel deals with the life of
Fernando Fe, a man in search of perfection in his artistic and personal life. Like Wilhelm Meister, the protagonist of *Simbad* becomes attracted to the theater in all its manifestations: the voluble
actors and actresses, the difficult process of transforming simple
words into spoken magic to sway a noncommitted audience, and the
mystery of creating a play that would sway the public due to its
dramatic structure, thematic brilliance, sharp characterization, and
emotional tone. Never content with the simple success or acceptance of his plays, Fernando Fe spends his life working as artistic
director for the Teatro Universal in Buenos Aires, always belittling
his past achievements, always searching to create the immortal play
that would sum up his artistic essence in a dazzling, final gesture.
Fe, not unlike his creator, pursues a myth shrouded in the very
mystery of the creative genius. Thus Mallea can state in retrospect:

"*Simbad* is the story—a terrible story—of the ironic and at the same time tragic event concerning the persecution of a myth . . . where the hunter is being caught by another hunter superior to himself. . . . The other aspect has to do with the tragedy of the creative act itself . . . creative activity hides an enormous mystery, a problem of an infinite dramatic transcendence."[46]

The act of creating, then, takes on a special significance for Mallea who was influenced by the Russian Berdyaev and his concept of the creative act as brought about partially by an element of absolute freedom that lies outside of the physical or metaphysical world.[47] This concept allows Mallea to return to the position of a free agent who must follow his inner dictates when exercising the somewhat esoteric art of writing. As a free agent he was justified to expand his inner self along the seven hundred and fifty pages of the novel and derive a psychological gratification from this process. Thus he was able to conceive the novel as a projection of his accumulated experience and inner vision without subjecting the lengthy work to a critical analysis as to form and structure. Mallea confides that "the main issues of this novel not only fascinated me but also entertained me greatly. The work produced an emotion in me that few other works of mine have been able to do. I visualized the scenes and relived the characters' experiences in such real terms that the whole business moved me as I have never been moved before."[48] Mallea issued himself a license to roam in the inner chambers of his mind and let rememberances and impressions flow and mingle copiously and freely.

The reader is taken to Bahía Blanca to witness the childhood and adolescence of Fernando Fe taking place in the seaport that appears so prominently in *The Enemies of the Soul* and even in *History of an Argentine Passion*. The protagonist Fernando Fe, like Mallea born in 1903, shares some of the latter's early experiences. He attends an English grammar school, walks along Avenida Colón, frequents the Londres Tea Room and the Marina Bar, and holds long conversations with classmates. After the death of his father and then his mother, Fe moves to Buenos Aires, writes plays, enters the world of the theater, and establishes a way of life not unlike that of most Mallean urban protagonists. There are two women in Fe's life; he will marry one, almost out of duty, and love the other until she decides to end their long affair. Somehow the great riddle of what life is all about is not answered by the force of love, the lure of the theater, or any other relationship. Rather, Fernando Fe chases an elusive intellectual ideal throughout most of the pages of this long novel.

He never stopped dreaming about finishing a great work, a noble one, a work that would serve as a justification for any human life. He could not stop dreaming that some day he would fulfill his childhood dreams: stimulating a sense of greatness and beauty in everybody . . . an admirable and important task, one that would make other people recognize him as an artist-benefactor, a man to whom they would owe much pleasure, emotion, meditation, the noblest thoughts. . . . No, he could never abandon his dream, no matter what. It made him feel good; very good.[49]

Fernando Fe, misunderstood by the public and the critics alike, finally hits upon the theme that seems to promise final success: Sindbad's eighth voyage in which he was to discover the gift of happiness, this most desirable of human achievements. While the dramatization of this theme eludes him, he does manage to embody Sindbad in his quest to reach beyond his own capabilities. The final page of the novel confirms Fernando Fe's transcendental attempt as a passerby calls out to him: "¡Adios, Simbad!"[50]

Fe's quest as well as the *porteño* background were no doubt very dear to Mallea who, by his own admission, savored the circumstances of his protagonist's sally into life and derived a vicarious pleasure from following in his footsteps. What remains debatable is whether the average reader can be expected to share the amorphous personal world constructed so minutely by and apparently for the author.

CHAPTER 5

The Last Epoch

AFTER the fall of the Perón regime in 1955 some of the major liberal writers—that is to say, the ones who had not compromised with the *justicialista* government—received their reward. Jorge Luis Borges, for instance, was given the prestigious post of director of the Biblioteca Nacional, the equivalent of the Library of Congress, a position he held until the advent of the second *peronista* era that began in 1973. Mallea was offered the ambassadorship to neighboring Uruguay, at that time in traditionally democratic hands. He refused that offer but subsequently agreed to represent Argentina as ambassador-at-large before UNESCO at its headquarters in Paris. In the decade following World War II the educational and cultural activities of UNESCO were surrounded by an aura of international prestige, and Mallea accepted the offer, although it cost him the editorship of *La Nación*'s "Literary Supplement" and thus a certain loss of influence over the local literary milieu.

With this appointment Mallea virtually reached the pinnacle of his lengthy literary career as far as public recognition was concerned. He had published a large number of novels, essays, and stories, some of which saw many printings. In 1945 he had received the Primer Premio Nacional de Letras and in the following year the Gran Premio de Honor of the Sociedad Argentina de Escritores, among whose members figure the country's most distinguished authors. Now in 1955 his novel *The Waiting Room* earned him the coveted Casavalle Prize. On the international scene several of his works came out in translation. *Fiesta in November, The Bay of Silence, The City on the Motionless River,* and *All Green Shall Perish* were introduced to the American and European public. In later years other works like *Chaves* and *The Ice Ship* were added to this list. *All Green Shall Perish* and *Chaves* also appeared in text editions in England and the United States respectively.

Beginning in 1956, Mallea spent over two years in the French capital working with his accustomed dedication and seriousness for the Cultural Affairs Board of UNESCO, and he was yet to enjoy a totally different experience when attending a conference in New Delhi, spending some forty days in what must have been an exciting encounter with the Orient—an experience later reflected in two of his novels. Needless to say, Mallea the writer did not remain idle, even before his return to Buenos Aires.

However, Mallea's next round of novels, collection of stories or *nouvelles,* and volumes of what might be called *pensées* unfortunately did not strike out in any new direction. Indicative of this static condition is his reference concerning the state of the modern novel. In his two volumes entitled *The Crossings (Las Travesías)* published in 1961 and 1962, respectively, he describes recent impressions of Europe and India and also takes issue, as he did in parts of *The Power of the Novel (Poderío de la novela),* with the problem of the novel as an adequate vehicle to record the changing social and technological patterns that affect modern man and his psyche. Thus he writes

It is not true that we are witnessing today the decay of the novel. Whatever changes actively in form does not present decay . . . the novel of our times tends to show a more introspective mood. It presents a more essay-like quality. It can also be considered to be a novel of knowledge because the conflicts generated by knowledge are in essence conflicts of intelligence; and this dramatization can but appeal to the modern reader.[1]

Quite obviously Mallea here shows his faith in the novel as a support for an intellectual speculation that is usually reserved for the essayistic mode. This point of view actually places Mallea closer to the novelistic concept held by members of the "Generation of '98" than that of the modern Latin American writers in search of a *nouveau roman.* The *desligamiento* between Mallea's novelistic tradition and the literary trends of the 1960's becomes quite pronounced and also aggravated by an instinctive insistence on repeating themes and establishing types that the reader has met before. His ensuing production falls into the accustomed categories of essayistic prose and fiction, mainly the latter.

In the former category we find *The Sterile Life (La vida blanca,* 1960), *The Inner War (La guerra interior,* 1963), *The Power of the*

Novel (Poderío de la novela, 1965), and *Gabriel Andaral* (1971) although it is listed as a novel. While *The Sterile Life* basically reintroduces the motif of the need for a national culture based on values steeped in a nobility of spirit and healthy traditions as previously defined in *History of an Argentine Passion, The Inner War* and *The Power of the Novel* alternate between commentaries on his earlier works and reflections on American and some European writers belonging mainly to the earlier part of the century.

On the fictional level Mallea clings to what seems to appear as a Golden Age of stylistic expression and mode of behavior. As he postulates in *The Sterile Life:* "Parallel to what happened on the level of history, the language of our forefathers has lost its impact, it has lost its voice, like everything else, and remains ignored and mutilated. There is no teaching in our metropolis that tries to save our linguistic profile or its authentic voice."[2]

True to this sentiment, the collections of stories *Possession (Posesión,* 1958), the three novelettes included in *The Resentment (El resentimiento,* 1966), the nine *relatos* in *The Ice Ship (La barca de hielo,* 1967), and most of the mini-stories from *The Net (La red,* 1968) constitute the efforts of a raconteur who seemingly entertains himself by developing anecdotal situations in an almost classical manner and style. In fact, the stories comprising *The Ice Ship* actually represent tales passed down to the author by members of his family.[3] His last two novels, told by the protagonist Adhemar Rivas who in *The Ice Ship* narrated Mallea's vicarious reminiscences, *The Penultimate Door (La penúltima puerta,* 1969) and its sequel, *Sad Skin of the Universe (Triste piel del universo,* 1971), reveal a romantically colored hero stewing in the juices of *Weltschmerz* whether staring into the muddy waters of the Paraná river, the Seine, or the Ganges, caught in a "love story" altered by an ever-present feeling of cosmic sadness.

As was to be expected, the critics slowly but surely began to register the widening gulf that began to separate the author of *The Bay of Silence* from the reading public brought up on magic realism and lately involved with such sociopolitical realities as the guerrilla movement and cultural imperialism. Especially the weeklies and popular magazines felt the need to strike a responsive chord in their readers and treated Mallea's new efforts with undue harshness. Thus the magazine *Confirmado* reviewed *The Penultimate Door* under the title of "Wilted Flowers" while pointing out the repetition of a sorrowful and sterile world that was so prevalent in his previous works.[4] But even the literary establishment was forced to take notice of Mallea's battle against the passage of time. In his review of *Sad Skin of the Universe* in which we find a disillusioned Adhemar Rivas in India, Mallea's successor at the helm of the "Literary Supplement" of *La Nación* affirmed that the novel was one of the better ones written by Mallea but that it was not a work that would appeal to the reader or even the critic of today.[5]

Probably the most competent summary of Mallea's writings from the point of view of the modern critic has been done by Emir Rodríguez Monegal.[6] Rodríguez Monegal traces the literary trajectory of Mallea, focusing first on his early and well-deserved triumphs, his major works such as *History of an Argentine Passion* and the *Bay of Silence*, pointing out his enormous influence over the Argentine literary scene until the advent of *peronismo* in 1945 and giving him due credit for exposing an Argentine national malaise in spite of turning out to be a better historian than prophet when it came to diagnosing currents that were to crystallize in a *peronista* spirit.[7] After 1945, however, the emerging newer generation, the *parricidas*, began to question Mallea's insistence on apparently unresolvable propositions and thus also began eroding, little by little, the layers of erudition and psychological attitudes that permeate so many of his characterizations, thoughts, and situations. This process ranged from a well-intentioned reproach by H. A. Murena of Mallea's analytic as well as syntactic estrangement from reality to a truly ferocious attack by the younger critic León Rozitchner. The latter not only sketched Mallea as a nostalgic bourgeois gentleman who, instead of passion and commitment, borrowed rhetoric from thinkers like Pascal or Kierkegaard; but Rozitchner also delighted in peeling off the masks of Mallea the rebel, the traveler, the lyric writer, or the philosopher.[8]

Yet it is Mallea himself who in the beginning of *The Penultimate Door* reveals a state of despair and insufficiency that underscores his genuine concern for his craft and attempts to find reasons for his failure to instill the essence of his spiritual crisis and his unique world through the magic of the written word.

No one seems to feel, as I do, the sadness and sterility of the shadow that eclipses my spirit . . . the sentiment that I shall never be able to write anything pleasing to myself and feeling that all my efforts are in vain because I shall not be able to tell what life has offered me and ordered for me, and thus I always feel impoverished due to my inability to make use of the spellbinding power of the human voice.[9]

To a large extent, then, the explanation of Mallea's need to use a minor key, to play up his cosmic sadness resides in his immense need to transcend his hermetic state and to look for a language and structure that would allow him to create in the reader an emotive response which would parallel his own feelings. In spite of the impact left by the essayistic proclamations that run through *History of an Argentine Passion* and the intellectual brilliance found in *The Bay of Silence* and similar novels, *All Green Shall Perish, Chaves,* and partially *Sindbad* are the works in which he was able to portray these feelings with conviction and artistry.

In 1970 Eduardo Mallea won the Gran Premio of the Fondo Nacional de las Artes, a distinction previously only awarded to two other Argentine writers, the poet Enrique Banchs and Jorge Luis Borges. Presently a number of his novels continue to be translated, and some of his essays have been used as texts in Argentine universities.

In spite of the nation's return to *peronismo* in 1973 and the development of a local literary scene that seems largely inclined toward a socially militant position at the expense of experimental-artistic preoccupation, Mallea's incessant search for a human existence and expression that goes beyond a mechanistic and materialistic level of life dictated by the necessities of a crowded and technocratic society and its dehumanizing process has reserved for him a distinguished and permanent place in the literature of his native country as well as abroad. In his best pages, the frailty, the frustration, and the agony of his protagonists, who so clearly reflect their creator, embody the nobility of succumbing in the Darwinian struggle of the expansion and triumph of the individual will at the expense of others. Mallea's answer to the insoluble dilemma propounded by Schopenhauer's pessimistic doctrine of voluntarism was to affirm his own will through the written word. If he abused this procedure the attempt ought to be viewed as a tragic condition that binds the author to his creation in a unique and often admirable process of injecting his consciousness into an otherwise meaningless world of phenomena.

Notes and References

Chapter One

1. *Diálogo con Mallea* (Buenos Aires, 1969), p. 14. In the 1960s Victoria Ocampo began to publish a series of dialogues with such outstanding literary figures as Jorge Luis Borges and Eduardo Mallea.

2. In his dialogue with Victoria Ocampo he was able to confirm some early childhood impression of this visit, especially of such places as the hotel Maurice and the Tuilleries in Paris; see ibid., p. 36.

3. *Obras completas*, vol. I (Buenos Aires, 1961), p. 315; hereafter cited as *OC*, I or II (Buenos Aires, 1965). All translations, unless otherwise indicated, are mine.

4. *OC*, I, 314.

5. *OC*, I, 315.

6. "Notas para Lewald," p. 1. These signed *Notas*, dating from 1971, comprise thirteen pages and were typed with handwritten changes as a supplement to some of my queries regarding biographical circumstances. The "Notas" are in my possession. From here on in, they will be referred to simply as "Notas."

7. *Diálogo con Mallea*, p. 18.

8. "Notas," p. 1.

9. Ibid.

10. Ibid.

11. Ibid., p. 2.

12. José Manuel Topete, "Eduardo Mallea y el laberinto de la agonía," *Revista Iberoamericana* 39 (1955), 120–21. See also Carmen Rivelli, *Eduardo Mallea, la continuidad temática de su obra* (New York, 1969), p. 16.

13. Ibid., p. 121.

14. Ibid.

15. *Diálogo con Mallea*, p. 37.

16. "Notas," p. 2.

17. *Los martinfierristas* (Buenos Aires, 1961), p. 25.

18. Prologue to Eduardo Mallea's *OC*, I, 9.

19. Ibid., p. 130.

20. *The Writings of Eduardo Mallea* (Berkeley, 1959), pp. 7–8.
21. See *OC*, I, 25.
22. *OC*, I, 51.
23. *OC*, I, 52–53.
24. *OC*, I, 48.

Chapter Two

1. "Notas," p. 2.
2. "Notas," p. 4.
3. *Diálogo con Mallea.*
4. *OC*, I, 66.
5. *OC*, I, 68.
6. *OC*, I, 70.
7. *OC*, I, 72.
8. *OC*, I, 77.
9. *OC*, I, 78.
10. *OC*, I, 86.
11. *OC*, I, 88.
12. *OC*, I, 104.
13. *OC*, I, 90.
14. *OC*, I, 133.
15. *OC*, I, 140.
16. *OC*, I, 140–41.
17. *OC*, I, 142.
18. *OC*, I, 84.
19. "Las últimas abras de Mallea," *Sur* 21, (1936), p. 65.
20. *OC*, I, 89–90.
21. *OC*, I, 90.
22. *Sur*, 12, (1935) pp. 7–29.
23. Bianco, pp. 69–71.
24. (Buenos Aires, 1963), p. 43.
25. See Mallea's own comments on what he calls "nine long years of silence" in *The Inner War*, p. 37.
26. *La guerra interior*, p. 37.
27. See, for instance, José M. Topete, "Eduardo Mallea y el laberinto de la agonia," *Revista Ibéroamericana*, 39 (1955), 131.
28. "La inquietud de Buenos Aires en la literatura argentina contemporánea," *Nosotros* 41 (1939), 357.
29. (Buenos Aires, 1954), pp. 11–13.
30. Ibid., p. 45.
31. *La ciudad junto al río inmóvil*, p. 26.
32. Ibid., p. 48.
33. Ibid., p. 55.
34. Ibid.

35. Ibid., p. 84.
36. Ibid., p. 89.
37. Ibid., p. 98.
38. Ibid.
39. Ibid., p. 109.
40. Ibid., p. 132.
41. *The Writings of Eduardo Mallea*, p. 49.
42. Ibid., pp. 57–58.
43. See Polt, p. 49.
44. "Notas," p. 4.
45. *OC*, I, 308.
46. *OC*, I, 330.
47. *OC*, I, 343.
48. *OC*, I, 347–48.
49. *OC*, I, 351.
50. *OC*, I, 352–53.
51. *OC*, I, 355.
52. *OC*, I, 356.
53. *OC*, I, 357.
54. *OC*, I, 388.
55. *OC*, I, 373.
56. See R. Scalabrini Ortiz, *El hombre que está solo y espera* (Buenos Aires, 1931), and P. Orgambide, *Yo, argentino* (Buenos Aires, 1968).
57. *OC*, I, 413.
58. *OC*, I, 419.
59. *History of an Argentine Passion*, p. 80.
60. *OC*, I, 428.
61. *OC*, I, 436.
62. *Sur*, 38 (1937), 81.

Chapter Three

1. "Fiesta en noviembre," *Sur*, 44 (1938), 66.
2. *OC*, I, 479–80.
3. *OC*, I, 506.
4. *OC*, I, 512–13.
5. *OC*, I, 514.
6. *OC*, I, 512.
7. See Ann Berry's review-article of *Fiesta en noviembre* that appeared in *Sur*, 47 (1938), especially pages 86–87.
8. *OC*, I, 524.
9. Francisco Ayala, "Meditación en la costa," *Sur*, 65 (1940), p. 104.
10. *OC*, I, 549.
11. *OC*, I, 551.
12. *OC*, I, 555.

13. *OC*, I, 576.
14. *OC*, I, 579.
15. *OC*, I, 578.
16. *OC*, I, 564.
17. See H. Ernest Lewald, *The Cry of Home* (Knoxville, 1972), p. 11.
18. *OC*, I, 580.
19. Patrick Dudgeon, *Eduardo Mallea. A personal study of his work* (Buenos Aires, 1949), pp. 31–32.
20. Ibid., p. 32.
21. Ibid., p. 33.
22. Mallea himself has been a member of this club for a number of years. The membership consists largely of what could still be called "landed gentry."
23. Dudgeon, p. 36.
24. *"La bahía de silencio,"* *Sur*, 75 (1940), 152.
25. Ibid., p. 153.
26. Polt, p. 103.
27. Canal Feijóo, *Sur*, 75 (1940), 154–55.
28. Polt, p. 103
29. *Breve historia de la literatura hispanoamericana* (Mexico City, 1959), p. 232.
30. Ibid., p. 233.
31. Ibid.
32. *Themen, Bilder, Motive im Werke Eduardo Malleas* (Geneva, 1966).
33. "Notas," p. 5.
34. Gillessen, p. 11.
35. Ibid., p. 18.
36. Ibid., pp. 16–31, passim.
37. Ibid., p. 30.
38. See especially Donald L. Shaw, "Narrative Technique in Mallea's *La bahía de silencio*," *Symposium* 20, no. 1 (1966), 54.
39. *OC*, I, 722.
40. *OC*, I, 732.
41. Shaw, p. 55.
42. Ibid., p. 33.
43. Ibid., p. 54.
44. See H. Ernest Lewald, "The Theme of Eduardo Mallea in *La bahía de silencio*," *Hispania*, 40 (1957), 177–78.
45. *OC*, I, 584.

Chapter Four

1. "Notas," p. 5.
2. Ibid.
3. Ibid.

4. Ibid.
5. Ibid.
6. *OC*, I, 995–96.
7. *OC*, I, 995.
8. "Man Trapped by Tension," *Saturday Review of Literature*, May 27, 1967, p. 32.
9. *OC*, I, 1038.
10. *OC*, I, 1046.
11. *OC*, I, 1071.
12. (Oxford, 1968), p. xxvi.
13. Gillessen, pp. 39–42.
14. "Notas," p. 13.
15. Ibid.
16. Review of *Las águilas*, *Sur*, 115 (1944), pp. 93–94.
17. *OC*, II, 71.
18. *OC*, II, 94.
19. See especially *El pecado original de América* (Buenos Aires, 1967), pp. 158–61.
20. *OC*, II, 28.
21. *OC*, II, 112.
22. "Notas," p. 6.
23. See "Carta a Eduardo Mallea," *Sur*, 197 (1951), pp. 38–43.
24. "Notas," pp. 6–7.
25. Ibid, p. 7.
26. *OC*, II, 455.
27. "Carta a Eduardo Mallea," p. 43.
28. "Contestación a González Lanuza," pp. 45–46.
29. Review of "La torre," *Sur*, 202 (1951), p. 59.
30. *OC*, II, 644.
31. Ibid.
32. Ibid.
33. *OC*, II, 60.
34. *Chaves* (Buenos Aires, 1953), p. 30.
35. Ibid., pp. 58–59.
36. Ibid., p. 84.
37. Ibid., p. 97.
38. "Chaves: un giro copernicano," *Sur*, 228 (1954), p. 32.
39. Ibid., p. 33.
40. *La guerra interior*, p. 80.
41. Review of "La sala de espera," *Sur*, 228 (1954), p. 98.
42. *La sala de espera* (Buenos Aires, 1957), p. 95.
43. Ibid., p. 102.
44. "Notas," p. 7.
45. Ibid., p. 8.

46. *La guerra interior*, pp. 80–81.
47. Ibid., p. 81.
48. "Notas," p. 8.
49. *Simbad* (Buenos Aires, 1957), p. 219.
50. Ibid., p. 746.

Chapter Five

1. *Las Travesías*, vol. 2 (Buenos Aires, 1962), p. 98.
2. *La vida blanca* (Buenos Aires, 1960), p. 81. In the preface to this work Mallea declares that it was to have come out in 1942 but that he followed an impulse not to present it to the reader at that time. Eighteen years later he decided that this portrayal of national-cultural problems belonging to the 1940s was indeed still valid enough to be published.
3. Mallea actually states in a subsequent work that much of the material for *La barca de hielo* had been provided to him by his aunt Romilia and two old ladies named Laura and Remigios who knew Mallea's family history. (See *La penúltima puerta*, p. 13.)
4. Unsigned review, *Confirmado*, January 21, 1970, p. 48.
5. Jorge Cruz, *La Nación*, February 6, 1972.
6. "Eduardo Mallea visible e invisible," in *Narradores de esta América*, vol. 1, E. Rodriguez Monegal, (Montevideo, 1969), pp. 249–69.
7. Ibid., pp. 249–54.
8. Ibid., pp. 256, 265–66.
9. *La penúltima puerta*, p. 9.

Selected Bibliography

PRIMARY SOURCES

Cuentos para una inglesa desesperada. Buenos Aires: Gleizer, 1926. A new edition with a prologue by the author and the inclusion of a new story, "Posesión," appeared in 1941, published by Espasa-Calpe.

Conocimiento y expresión de la Argentina. Buenos Aires: Sur, 1935.

Nocturno europeo. Buenos Aires: Sur, 1935.

La ciudad junto al río inmóvil. Buenos Aires: Sur, 1936.

Historia de una pasión argentina. Buenos Aires: Sur, 1937. A new edition with a prologue by Francisco Romero was brought out by Espasa-Calpe in 1940.

Fiesta en noviembre. Buenos Aires: Amigos del Libro Argentino, 1938.

Meditación en la costa. Buenos Aires: Imprenta Mercatali, 1939.

La bahía de silencio. Buenos Aires: Sudamericana, 1940.

Todo verdor perecerá. Buenos Aires: Espasa-Calpe, 1941.

Las águilas. Buenos Aires: Sudamericana, 1943.

Rodeada está de sueño. Buenos Aires: Espasa-Calpe, 1944.

El retorno. Buenos Aires: Espasa-Calpe, 1946.

Los enemigos del alma. Buenos Aires: Sudamericana, 1950.

La torre. Buenos Aires: Sudamericana, 1951.

Chaves. Buenos Aires: Losada, 1953.

La sala de espera. Buenos Aires: Sudamericana, 1953.

Simbad. Buenos Aires: Sudamericana, 1957.

Posesión. Buenos Aires: Sudamericana, 1958. Four short novels.

La vida blanca. Buenos Aires: Sur, 1960.

Las Travesías. Vol. 1. Buenos Aires: Sudamericana, 1961.

Las Travesías. Vol. 2. Buenos Aires: Sudamericana, 1962.

La guerra interior. Buenos Aires: Sur, 1963.

El resentimiento. Buenos Aires: Sudamericana, 1966. Three short novels.

La barca de hielo. Buenos Aires: Sudamericana, 1967. Nine stories.

La red. Buenos Aires: Sudamericana, 1968.

La penúltima puerta. Buenos Aires: Sudamericana, 1969.

Gabriel Andaral. Buenos Aires: Sudamericana, 1971.

Triste piel del universo. Buenos Aires: Sudamericana, 1971.

Obras completas. Vol. 1. Buenos Aires: Emecé, 1961. Contains *Cuentos para una inglesa desesperada, Conocimiento y expresión de la Argentina, Nocturno europeo, La ciudad junto al río inmóvil, Historia de una pasión argentina, Fiesta en noviembre, Meditación en la costa, La bahía de silencio, Todo verdor perecerá,* and *El sayal y la púrpura.*

Obras completas. Vol. 2. Buenos Aires: Emecé, 1965. Contains *Las águilas, Rodeada está de sueño, El retorno, El vínculo, Los enemigos del alma,* and *La torre.*

SECONDARY SOURCES

1. Books

ALEGRÍA, FERNANDO. *Breve historia de la novela hispanoamericana.* Mexico: De Andrea, 1959. Pp. 231–36. An appraisal of Mallea's main traits and characters. Good synopsis.

DUDGEON, PATRICK. *Eduardo Mallea. A Personal Study of his Work.* Buenos Aires: Agonia, 1949. A brief study, mainly focused on *Fiesta en noviembre* and *La bahía de silencio.*

GILLESSEN, HERBERT. *Themen, Bilder und Motive im Werk Eduardo Malleas.* Kölner Romanistische Arbeiten, heft 36. Geneva: Librairie Droz, 1966. Unquestionably the most serious study of Mallea's symbols, characters, and literary sources.

LICHTBLAU, MYRON I. *El arte estilístico de Eduardo Mallea.* Buenos Aires: Goyanarte, 1967. As the title indicates, a study of the author's style and language including his best-known works. A fine and systematic effort.

OCAMPO, VICTORIA. *Diálogo con Mallea.* Buenos Aires: Sur, 1969. The famous Argentine woman writer and longtime editor-owner of *Sur* reminisces with Mallea. Some valuable biographical insights.

POLT, JOHN H. R. *The Writings of Eduardo Mallea.* Berkeley: University of California Press, 1959. A published doctoral dissertation that has an "all-around" approach to Mallea's works through the mid-1950s. It focuses on fiction as well as on such important essays as *Historia de una pasión argentina.*

RIVELLI, CARMEN. *Eduardo Mallea. La continuidad temática de su obra.* New York: Las Americas Publishing Company, 1969. An in-depth analysis of Mallea that recreates the main cultural and intellectual preoccupations of the author. Also has a good chapter on style.

2. Articles and Reviews

AYALA, FRANCISCO. "Meditación en la costa." *Sur* 65 (1940), 100–106.

BERRY, ANN. "Fiesta en noviembre." *Sur* 57 (1939), 81–87.

BIANCO, JOSÉ. "Las últimas obras de Mallea." *Sur* 21 (1936), 39–71. Special emphasis on the essayistic works, *Nocturno europeo* and *La ciudad junto al río inmóvil.*

BULLRICH, SILVINA. "La inquietud de Buenos Aires en la literatura argentina contemporánea." *Nosotros* 6, no. 41 (1939), 341–57. A well-known Argentine novelist looks at the big-city milieu and characters of Mallea.

CANAL FEIJÓO, BERNARDO. "Historia de una pasión argentina." *Sur* 38 (1937), 74–83.

————. "La bahía de silencio." *Sur* 75 (1940), 151–58. A frank commentary on the novel's shortcomings.

CHAPMAN, ARNOLD. "Terms of Spiritual Isolation in Eduardo Mallea." *Modern Language Forum* 37 (1952), 21–27. Focuses on Mallea's metaphoric language in his early works.

————. "Manuel Galvez y Eduardo Mallea." *Revista Iberoamericana* 19 (1937), 71–78.

CROW, JOHN A. "Man Trapped by Tension." *Saturday Review*, May 27, 1967, pp. 32–33. Mainly an evaluation of *Todo verdor perecerá*.

GONZÁLEZ LANUZA, EDUARDO. "Carta a Eduardo Mallea." *Sur* 197 (1951), 38–48. A critique of *Los enemigos del alma*, followed by a reply by Mallea on pp. 43–48.

LEWALD, H. ERNEST. "El tema de Eduardo Mallea en *La bahía de silencio.*" In *Iberoamérica*, Robert G. Mead, ed., pp. 108–12, Mexico: De Andrea, 1962.

MONEGAL, EMIR RODRÍGUEZ. *Narradores de esta América.* Montevideo: Alfa, 1969. Vol. 1, pp. 249–69. A very modern and critical approach to Mallea as a subjective force in his dealings with Argentine culture.

MURENA, H. A. "Chaves: un giro copernicano." *Sur* 208 (1952), 27–36.

SHAW, DONALD L. Introduction to *Todo verdor perecerá* by Eduardo Mallea. Oxford: Pergamon Press, 1968, pp. vii–xxxiii. An outstanding analysis of this work.

————. "Narrative Technique in Mallea's *La bahía de silencio.*" *Symposium* 20 (1966), 50–55.

SOTO, LUIS EMILIO. "La torre." *Sur* 202 (1951), 53–60.

————. "Las águilas." *Sur* 115 (1944), 88–94.

TOPETE, JOSÉ M. "Eduardo Mallea y el laberinto de la agonía." *Revista Iberoamericana* 39 (1955), 117–49. A partially biographical study of Mallea's earlier works and an evaluation of his existentialist tendencies.

Index